The Power In Ageing

A LIFE-STAGE GUIDE

Adam Duncan

Copyright © 2023 Adam Duncan

All rights reserved.

No part of this publication may be reproduced, stored or transmitted in any form or by any means, electronic, mechanical, photocopying, recording, scanning, or otherwise without written permission from the publisher. It is illegal to copy this book, post it to a website, or distribute it by any other means without permission.

Adam Duncan asserts the moral right to be identified as the author of this work.

Adam Duncan has no responsibility for the persistence or accuracy of URLs for external or third-party Internet Websites referred to in this publication and does not guarantee that any content on such Websites is, or will remain, accurate or appropriate.

ISBN 9798865724438

FEEDBACK FROM LIFE-STAGE COURSES

I have so much gratitude for the encouragement and help. For me the course was a homecoming, a sense of belonging. It is such a powerful thing to be listened to and feel heard. CECILIA DEVENNEY WALL

Thank you for a day that brought insights and understanding and the joy of sharing , listening and growing in the company of others. LOUCINDA MIDGLEY

It's hugely important for me as an older man to re-engage with my peers, and with this time of life, positively. Life-Stage offers me a creative, safe and beneficial way to do that." DAVID PUGSLEY

I really enjoyed the event. This is such a rich community you are creating and I'm very pleased to be part of it. NICOLA GLINWOOD

In 2021, I helped Life-Stage organise a trial programme with 10 residents in Earlsdon Park Retirement Village. Many joined out of curiosity initially and stayed because they found it so fascinating. The videos and activities were engaging and the feedback was positive.. I strongly believe this programme can bring lasting value and benefit to communities. JOANNA FRANCIS, RESIDENT'S ASSOCIATION, EARLSDON RETIREMENT VILLAGE

ABOUT

This book is the result of workshops and on-line sessions that have been run by Life-Stage over the last five years. It is designed to help people in the second half of life find their inner wisdom and courage. It provides a method of transforming fears around ageing into deeper connection and purpose. The process enhances self-belief and resilience

There are limitations to developing our physical world as we grow older, but we can continue to develop a rich inner life to find joy and fulfilment.

The Power in Ageing is effective for people of all faiths or people of no faith.

CONTENTS

PREFACE ix
INTRODUCTION 1

PART 1: LIFE REVIEW

The Dependent Child 21
The Independent Adult 37
The Inter-Dependent Mature Adult 55
Transforming Fear 73

PART 2: THE SEED OF INTENTION

Why an Intention 89
Finding the Seed 105
Tending the Shoots: 133
Harvesting the Fruits 139

PART 3: NOTES

PREFACE

I've discovered that you need wisdom and courage to deal with the challenges of ageing. No matter how wealthy or healthy you are, it is hard to fully enjoy the benefits of a long life without these two qualities.

Five years ago I thought I was more foolish than wise. I considered myself quite fearful – not a total wimp, but certainly not courageous. But around this time, I had two experiences that changed my life – two events that are common to most people over a certain age.

The Death of a Parent

My mother lay asleep in the hospice. She was dying slowly. Fighting as she always had done, and not wanting to let go. It is a remarkable to witness the person who gave me life, ending theirs. I felt fearful and emotionally ill-equipped.

The hospice was like nowhere I'd been before. This was a place devoted to the dying and yet surprisingly, it didn't feel depressing. There was an air of tranquillity where medics, nurses and volunteers went about their business with calm, good humour as though dying was the most natural thing in the world. Although I felt emotional about the end of my mother's life, I also felt reassured that she had good people caring for her.

I waited all morning hoping to connect with my sleeping mother. At lunchtime I went to the shopping centre to get something to eat in the canteen of a department store. After I bought a sandwich and a cup of tea, I noticed the cashier. It was as though all the life had been drained out of this woman. She was on autopilot. She was probably in her forties but to me, in my heightened emotional state, the cashier looked as though she had died a long time ago.

While I ate my sandwich, I looked around the canteen and what I saw was quite shocking. It seemed as though the place was full of the undead. It felt as though there was no humanity here in the shopping centre. There were just functional efficiencies and bleak transactions. From where I was sitting, the staff and the customers in the canteen all looked like extras in a zombie film. There was neither life nor death in the shopping centre. Just the undead. I wanted to get back to the love and compassion in the hospice - where life and death were acknowledged. Where people were valued no matter what state they were in.

Retirement

After my mother's death, I started reviewing what I had done with my life and what I wanted to do with the time I had left. For the last ten years, I'd put a lot of energy into working with a charity called *A Band of Brothers* (ABOB) doing rites-of-passage weekends for young men in the Criminal Justice System. The purpose was to help them move on from adolescent behaviour to healthy masculinity. It was powerful and rewarding mentoring work around life-transition. A group of us would go to the woods on a Thursday to prepare the physical and emotional ground for fifteen or so young men to arrive on Friday. Most of the young men went home on Sunday evening with the hope of a new beginning in their lives and a willingness to be mentored into healthy community. I loved the challenge of the work, the processes we used as well as the camaraderie of building a healthy community together.

However, there was a problem. At the age of 70, I was finding the long days and nights camping in the woods with a demanding schedule that sometimes didn't finish until after midnight, too much. Of course, I didn't want to admit it. I tried to keep up with my 'brothers' who I generally considered to be my contemporaries, but they were often thirty years younger! What I could do when I was sixty-five, was no longer possible. I would sometimes take on the 'elder' role, but the physicality was proving too much for me. I fell over and broke a rib at the start of one session and felt I was failing myself, my colleagues and the young men. There was shame at being too old to fully participate, though I was never going to publicly admit it.

I would still turn up for meetings, but I started to feel critical about the work and I would long for the event to end. The feeling of connection and joy that I had felt for many years had gone and I felt huge grief at the thought of losing my 'tribe'. I had spent nearly ten years of my life contributing to the community and now I felt alone and passed it. Like many people who have to retire from the work they love, I felt like this was the beginning of a slow decline to the end of my life. These were dark times for me. The joy of life had gone but it was in this darkness that a new seed started to germinate.

Fresh Perspective

What did my growing old mean? Was I passed it? What was my purpose. I could no longer pretend to be middle-aged. I realised how unaccepting I was of the ageing process and how unprepared I was for this stage of life. Why was I surprised to be this old? The idea of fully accepting my age was a challenging one, but I started to explore how I could shed my old skin and move forward into a new stage of life.

As luck would have it, I was offered a place on a course with an organisation called Living Well Dying Well.

With some work, I started to come to terms with my own mortality. I was able to let go of some of the old attachments and this gave me a new lease of life and a surge of creative energy that I hadn't felt for decades.

As I had been involved in helping young men transition from adolescence to healthy adulthood, I started to wonder if there wasn't a need for another transition in later life. I did some research and talked to some wise elders - men and women who were fearlessly committed to not stagnating in later life. I discovered that within many indigenous communities, the process of marking key stages in life was seen as absolutely necessary for the well-being of the tribe.

In 2020, I started Life-Stage with the belief that later life offers the opportunity to explore inner wisdom and courage which are the qualities we need to age well. We are a small but growing community of 'elders-in-training' who are working to change the paradigm around ageing.

Adam Duncan

September 2023

INTRODUCTION

This book is for those who have experienced a good deal of life and have known some ups and downs. It is for those who have been through the storms of youth and of middle age.

You may still be in your late 40s and dealing with the cut and thrust of life or you may have retired a long time ago. You will have taken at least 400 million breaths so far and hope to take a lot more. You are a survivor with a wealth of life experience. You have known many losses. Your youth has long gone, and middle age has slipped over the horizon, and yet in your mind you are not old. You have ideas and thoughts that would have been beyond the scope of your immature brain.

In the second half of life[1], the ticking of the clock begins to get louder. Time seems to move faster now than in your youth. You see younger generations coming up behind you who think that anyone over 40 is ancient. They believe that sex, fashion and music

---

1 Only in retrospect can we say when the second half of life starts. The life span of men and women in the UK combined is 81.05 years which means that according to statistics the second half of life starts when you're a few months over 40. *Office of National Statistics*

are the exclusive preserve of their generation (just as you did at their age). As you have grown older, you have become more aware of the effects of ageing on the generations in front of you. The lively uncles and aunts of your childhood are now elderly or have died.

What now?

So, congratulations on making it this far! But the key question is, how do you make the most of each day in this phase of life? Surely there has to be more than just survival! How do you deal with your concerns around ageing, and what preparations can you make for a sparkling and dynamic end of life? How do you deal emotionally with this part of the journey? How do you let go of the past and find meaning in the present? How can you find enthusiasm for the future? This book is aimed at those who want to age with wisdom and courage in order to transform the fear of ageing.

Changing the Belief

The common perception of later life is that it is populated with sad and lonely people. Paul McCartney's song, Eleanor Rigby, was written in 1966 and it captures one of our deepest fears. *"Father McKenzie darning his socks in the night, when there's nobody there"* conjures up the isolation and hopelessness that is often associated with later life.

Many of the baby-boomers who sang along to that chorus all those decades ago are now approaching later life themselves. Most of us dread the thought of such a tragic ending to life. We see older people struggling and wonder what it must be like to be them. What will it be like for me? In the face of old age, many people feel that there is nothing they can do. They feel helpless, so they avoid thinking about it.

If you believe that ageing is about diminishment and suffering, then there is a strong chance that you will not age well. But what if there was another story? What if you could change the belief? Of course, it's natural to have concerns about growing older. But we are not powerless. Far from it! Some people come into their own as they age, others become depressed. Take the story of Ann and Charlotte, for example;

CHARLOTTE & ANN'S EXPERIENCE

The two sisters met at restaurant on the South Bank overlooking the Thames. They were celebrating Ann's 60th birthday. Just the two of them. There were kisses, hugs and a bottle of bubbly. Ann said she couldn't believe she was sixty. It seemed like only yesterday they were still at school. Ann was a year younger than Charlotte, though the sisters could have been twins. They lived in different towns, but they phoned each other regularly. They would meet for lunch every month or so, but that sixtieth birthday celebration overlooking the sunlit Thames was special for both of them.

Ten years later Charlotte was keen to celebrate Ann's 70th birthday at the restaurant again, but Ann didn't want to travel to London. Since her retirement, Ann had become less communicative. Eventually, Charlotte managed to drag her sister out for a meal. Even before they ordered, Ann started complaining. She didn't like eating out. She hated getting old and she certainly didn't want to celebrate her age. After a few glasses of wine, Ann admitted that she resented the way her sister's life was flourishing since her retirement and she hated how her own life seemed to be diminishing.

Some people like Ann are overwhelmed by the emotional turmoil that change in later life can create. A few, like Charlotte, experience an inner freedom as they grow older. Within the same family there can be a stark contrast between how people respond to the challenges of growing older. This book is about how you can flourish as you grow older.

Life changes

Retirement from work is just one of many changes that can affect us deeply in the second half of life. The loss of family or friends, the loss of physical or mental capacity, divorce, the menopause, living in an 'empty nest' or 'down-sizing' can all cause emotional distress. Such life changes can be deeply challenging to our sense of self and what we have to offer to the world. Many lose their self-confidence as they age. Others find a new way forward.

This book is designed to help you make a conscious choice about how you want to be now and in later life. The chapters take you through three stages of life development – from the dependent child, to the limited mind-set of the independent adult and then, towards the freedom of the inter-dependent, mature adult. It's a re-framing of the ageing journey and an opportunity to see what might prevent you from living a fulfilling life.

Negative Ageing

We see ageing as a problem that needs to be fixed rather than a natural function of life. In a society that prioritises wealth, fitness and appearances, we struggle with the whole concept of growing old. . Despite millions spent on research and the best efforts of numerous charities, the ageing problem looms larger than ever. The health and care services are overwhelmed. There's an epidemic of loneliness, and for many the future looks increasingly bleak. So, how do we develop our innate wisdom and courage to respond to ageing without fear?

When people are asked what they want in later life, they often responded with a negative. *I don't want to feel any pain. I don't want to be incapacitated. I don't want to be lonely.* Such responses are based on fear which is understandable, but if ageing well is about minimising the emotional and physical pain of growing older, you might say that someone in a coma is ageing very well indeed!

Addicted to More

Some people say you need to be wealthy to age well. But money and power often breed a hunger for more of the same. Rich people often dread the thought of having to part with the trappings of wealth. King Lear, for example, had everything ... except the wisdom to come to terms with his ageing. Shakespeare's tragedy is as relevant today as it was four hundred years ago. In the face of death, money and social standing mean nothing

Other people said that in retirement they wanted 'more' of something. More holidays. More comfort. More security. To acquire more. To achieve more. Many people around retirement age just wanted more time to stay looking and feeling young for as long as possible. While looking gorgeous and drinking cocktails on the beach might be the dream for some, it is not really a sustainable reality for most of us in later life!

A Sense of Purpose

Many academic research papers[2] point to a sense of purpose as being a key to wellbeing in later life. A sense of purpose implies that there is stuff to be done - learn new skills, plan a trip, decorate the house. Any of these activities might be said to give us a sense of

---

2 Ageing Well Groups 2017 OUP on behalf of the British Geriatrics Society

purpose. Doctors, gerontologists, physiotherapists all encourage us to keep active. Use it or lose it they say. Whatever it is you can do, do it. Just keep busy for as long as you can. While purpose has a role to play in ageing well, it has limitations.

A sense of purpose gives us energy and motivation. It can give us a sense of pride in what we do. But beware! It can be fickle. For example, a famous player set his sights on winning the Rugby World Cup. It was what gave his life purpose and meaning during all the hard years of training and commitment. After he achieved his aim and had received abundant praise and glory, the player became depressed. His motivation was gone and so had his life force. Everything in the wake of winning the World Cup, seemed small and insignificant. In the second half of life, we are especially prone to the loss of purpose, as Debbie's story shows.

DEBBIE'S EXPERIENCE

Debbie made a big decision to retire from a job that she enjoyed at the age of 59. She lost out financially, but she decided it was a sacrifice worth making for the sake of Rosie, her granddaughter.

When Rosie was twelve, her parents had an acrimonious divorce. Debbie was determined to do all in her power to make sure that Rosie got the support that she needed. As their relationship grew closer, it gave Debbie a sense of joy that she never quite felt while bringing up her own daughter.

By the time Rosie went to drama school at 19, they saw less of each other but the bond between the two was still strong. When Rosie bought a young Australian actor to have lunch, Debbie felt anxious, and the meeting did not go well. In the summer holidays, Rosie and her fella went to Australia to meet his people and they did not return in the Autumn to complete their training.

Now and again, Rosie and her grandmother had a Zoom call, but it often ended in tears. Debbie still had a small social life, but she felt she had lost her sense of purpose in life. There seemed little to get her out of bed in the morning other than to feed her faithful cat. Fortunately, on the eve of her 70th birthday, she was inspired by a friend to look at what was going on in her life and to see a bigger picture.

A sense of purpose is generally context bound. It is limited to a certain set of circumstances. While results-orientated thinking might have powered us through our time as a younger adult, in the second half of life, having a sense of purpose may not always be so effective. In later life it is worth exploring what's behind the purpose. What are the characteristics that drive the purpose? What is our intention?

Intention

As we get older it is easy to adopt patterns of habitual behaviour. We may start to live most of life unintentionally. We know what works for us and what doesn't. We know what we like and what we don't like. We don't need to be aware all the time. We don't need to think too much. If you were confronted with a terminal diagnosis and were asked how you wanted your remaining days to be, you would probably question some of your current behaviour patterns. It is a horrible cliché but we're all on a terminal diagnosis, though the end of life maybe years or decades away.

So how do you want to be at the end of your life? What if you had inner powers to draw on in the final moments? What if you could access great courage and wisdom from the depths of your being as you face a certain ending? What if you could look back at your life without regret and with a sense of appreciation for everything? If you've got to go (and you do), wouldn't you want access to this inner power?

Inner Resources

Of course, you can't buy this inner power on Amazon or anywhere else. You already have it. Whether you've lived a life of reckless debauchery or stoic discipline, we all carry an inner power within us. It's not in a sacred building, in a shaman or a guru. We won't find it on the mountain top or in a retreat centre. There is an inner power within each of us, no matter what our religious beliefs. The atheist, the agnostic and the worshipper all have it. It is a natural resource we human beings are fortunate to possess. And it is awesome! It may lie buried deep within us, or it may be close to the surface. It may be operational on a regular basis, or your true inner power may never have seen active service. No matter how great our triumphs and achievements, no matter our status or character, we come to a point in the second half of life where we would do well to look deeply at our vulnerability and mortality in order to find this treasure within.

The Quest

In many of the best fairy tales the hero or heroine needs to go on an arduous and dangerous journey to gain their reward and discover the treasure. After much hardship and travelling, they come to a place where they are severely tested. In the Russian fairy tales, it is often the witch Baba Yaga[3] who challenges the protagonist. There, in the middle of the vast forest is the grotesque old woman who represents a powerful force of nature. It is only when the heroine

---

3 *Russian Fairy Tales* (Illustrated) by Alexander Afanasyev (Author), The Planet; Illustrated Edition

confronts her deepest fears that she finds her way to true happiness.

In the stories and myths, it is in the darkest place that the protagonist discovers inner qualities that they didn't know they possessed. It seems a universal law of nature that if we accept the challenge of the quest, then the latent forces of the universe will challenge us but will ultimately support us on our journey if we don't give up. Without undergoing the journey, our inner power remains latent.

It is not the amount of time we have left on this earth, but what we do with it, that gives us power. To agonise over what steps we should take as we grow older and worry excessively about our demise makes us impotent. Health, money, fitness, diet; these things are important, but they are nothing compared to discovering our full life potential. Everyone has vast resources of courage, wisdom and compassion inside, but these qualities cannot be accessed with the handbrake on. It is only when we take action and stop living in fear that our highest qualities can be manifest. To age well we need the courage to face the unknown challenges of growing older. We need the wisdom to see the true nature of things and we need the compassion to take us out of the small self and to see the bigger picture. There are bound to be problems as we age, but each challenge can enable us to deepen confidence in our own power, so that we enjoy our journey without fear.

Before we begin this process, there is some important information about how to use this book and get the most from it.

THE COURSE

Part 1: Life Stage Development

Every one of us is unique. - even so-called identical twins! Humans share about 99% of the same genome but we tend to focus on the differences between us. Besides sharing much of the same genetic coding, we also share developmental experiences that are common to all of us.

The ageing process has been happening since conception but in the late afternoon of life we become increasingly aware of its physical and mental effects. This awareness can separate us if we get wrapped up in our own unique story. On the other hand there is a possibility that entropy and vulnerability can connect us on a deeper level. We each have a unique story, but how can we move on from our small individual self to something far greater?

In the first part of this book, we are going to look at some of the stages in our development that have got us to this point. From conception. To birth. To childhood. To adolescence. To young adult. To middle age and right up to right up to this present moment. This journey is our past and is part of who we are right now.

Part 2: A Life Intention

After reviewing your life journey up to the present time, we consider the bigger picture and what is really important to you at this stage in your life? We look at how we can manifest wisdom and courage to live a fulfilled life.

The book contains 10 questions about some profound aspects of your life which you are invited to answer. They are designed to give you some perspective and clarity about what is important to you right now. In the Life-Stage workshops, participants ponder on each question in silence, before writing down a few thoughts in their notebooks. The questions may bring up some feelings you are not used to. This is not therapy, so if you feel uncomfortable, move on to the next section and perhaps come back to it at a later date.

After each question there are some personal responses to some of the questions from members of the Life-Stage community.

Notebook and an Open Mind

You are encouraged to prepare yourself with a notebook in which to explore ideas and to help you reflect.

If you have kept a journal before, then you will be familiar with the benefits of this inner adventure. It helps to have an open mind and some patience if you want to get the best results.

Breathing

Breathing is the process of moving air into and from the lungs to facilitate gas exchange with the internal environment, mostly to flush out carbon dioxide and bring in oxygen.

We take breathing for granted but several clinical trials show how slow and conscious breathing effects autonomic functions such as blood pressure and heart rate.[4] Awareness of breath also helps us to come fully into the present moment.

The importance of breath awareness was recognised in ancient India where the word 'prana' not only meant breath but also 'the sacred essence of life'. In Chinese medicine 'chi' means breath as well as the universal and cosmic energy of life.

Today conscious breathing is frequently recommended for mental and emotional wellbeing. The pace of change and the speed of modern life is often overwhelming (even for younger generations), so it is worth getting into the habit of slowing things down with a few deliberate breaths.

Over the course of reading this book, you may take as many as 20,000 breaths.[5] While you are working your way through and answering the questions in the book, there will be the occasional reminder to become aware of your breathing. If you can stop to become conscious of your breath (even for a short time), it will make the experience of reading this book more powerful.

---

4 *Effect of short-term practice of breathing exercises on autonomic functions in normal human volunteers* Pal, GK S Velkumary, Madanmohan

5 The average person takes about 16 breaths per minute, or 960 breaths per hour, 23,040 breaths a day, 8,409,600 a year. If you lived to the age of 75, that would mean 630,720,000 breaths in your lifetime.

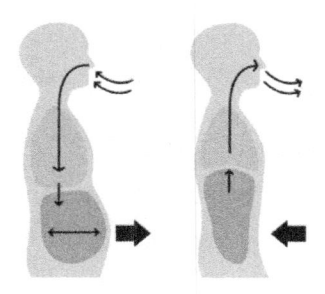

When you are invited to check in with your breathing, take three deeper breaths: breathing in slowly through your nose, allowing your chest and lower belly to rise as you fill your lungs. Let your abdomen expand fully. Now breathe out slowly through your mouth.

Case Studies

The book is not an academic study of ageing but is designed to be of practical use in the real world. Throughout the book there are some true personal experiences around different aspects of ageing. The names have been changed but each piece is based on actual events.

Community

And remember, you are not alone. There is a vibrant Life-Stage community with a free monthly on-line discussion forum, regular courses, workshops and one-to-one sessions available. For more information, go to www.life-stage.org

So, now we are going to start working towards a life intention by reflecting on life from the very beginning of our ageing process.

PART 1

LIFE STAGE DEVELOPMENT

*Youth is the gift of nature,
but age is a work of art.*
STANISLAW JERZY LEC

Dependent
CHILD

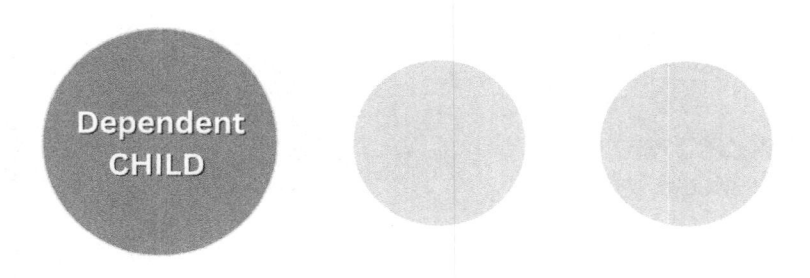

The Wonder of the Zygote

We did our most dynamic ageing before we were even born. Life for us began when a mature sperm entered the ovum. When the two united, they produced a zygote which is the smallest form of human life. Both the ovum and the sperm were single cells, each with a unique function, but the zygote was your life itself. That single cell contained much of the basic information that determines who you are now. What a wonder! Within the zygote you had 23 chromosomes from your mother and 23 from your father.

At four weeks, you had a beating heart, you looked like a tadpole and were about the size of a sesame seed! You were asleep for over 90% of your gestation in the womb. By the time you were born, that single cell zygote which contained your essence, had divided and grown into around 26 billion cells. Wonder upon wonder!

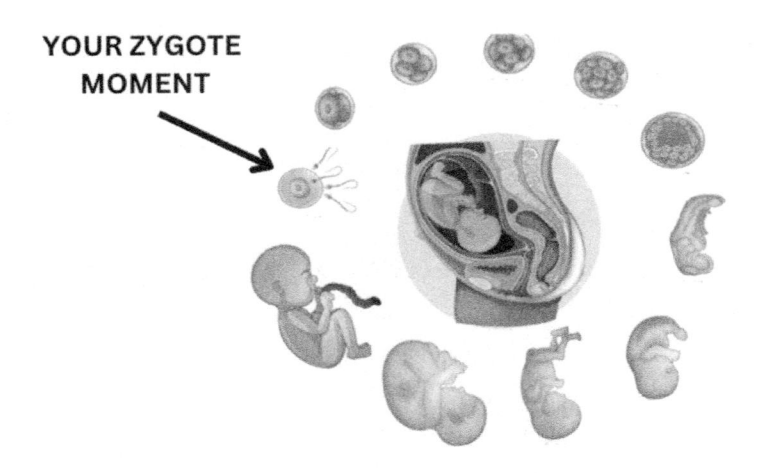

YOUR ZYGOTE MOMENT

Up until your first breath , you were totally dependent on your mother for your survival.

The invitation is not to rush ahead, but to take three conscious breaths to connect with the extraordinary miracle that is a momentous part of your history.

Baby

In your first year, you babbled and cooed and tried to imitate language. You crawled and learnt to focus your vision. You were reaching out to explore the world around you. The fingers and toes that you could wiggle were a wonder. You were learning fast as you developed memory, thinking, language and reasoning skills. The chances are that around the end of your first year, you first experienced the emotion of fear, some of which may have been learnt from observing the adults around you[6].

Child

Within a couple of years, you were a walking, talking toddler. As a child, time moved in slow motion. At five, one year was one fifth of your entire life. You saw things mostly in the short term and it took forever for birthdays to come around. Now, in later life, a year is a tiny fraction of your existence and the birthdays keep coming all too quickly! Back then, you had a small radius of perception of the world, with little awareness of the complex connections that ran through life and you were still mostly dependent on others for your basic physical and emotional needs.

If you were fortunate, you had the freedom to explore and play without too much inhibition. Your curiosity opened you up to the wonder and mystery of life. The newness of the world had many surprises and fresh

---

6 Research has shown that babies at around 8 – 12 months old understand the meaning of a fearful face and start to produce fearful expressions and other fear-based behaviours such as clinging to a parent and making distressed sounds.

sensations. The first covering of snow on the ground. Ripples on water. Autumn leaves blowing in the wind. The vastness of the sea. It was all new to you back then. And at the same time, you were learning language and social interaction with remarkable speed.

By the age of 6, you had developed coordination and balance. You were engaging in social situations and remarkably your brain had reach about 95% of its full adult size. The chances are your brain was bigger then than it is now!

By the time you were thirteen you had already passed many cognitive peaks such as the optimum time to learn a new language[7]. You were becoming more aware of the outside world and how you might fit into it.

---

7 Below are some optimum peak ages according to Chris Weller and Skye Gould; learning a new language is 7; brain processing power is 18 remembering names is 22; muscle strength is 25; running a marathon is 28;

QUESTION 1

This is the first of 10 questions that are designed to support you in gaining a fresh perspective and in ageing consciously. In order to get the most from the book, it is recommended that you read the question below, close your eyes, take a few deliberate breathes and reflect on the question. While you breath, see what comes to mind. If you can, allow any images or thoughts to come to you rather than chasing them.

Whatever emerges is fine. It may seem trivial or even cliched. Don't worry.

When you're ready, write a few words, sentences or paragraphs in your notebook about what came up for you.

What gave you a sense of wonder as a child?

Don't worry if nothing comes to mind. It may do later, in which case don't forget to make a note of it.

Once you have made your notes, you can see examples of responses from a few of the Life-Stage subscribers on the next page.

Some personal answers to QUESTION 1
"What gave you a sense of wonder as a child?"

Seeing tiny stick insects hatch from eggs that I had in a jar.

I was a toddler/pre-walker and have this strange memory of being chased up a drive by a turtle. Me on my hands and knees; the turtle chasing me.

Snow falling through the light of street lamps

I was about 4 years old when I accidentally let go of the balloon I was carrying. It floated up and kept on going. I was crying because I had lost my balloon, and I remember the exact moment I stopped and watched it drift away, I thought it would hit something and come back down again, I couldn't understand that my balloon could just keep going up.

When I saw the full moon out of my bedroom window one night. It seemed so close.

Rock pools. It seemed like it was another universe that I could touch. I felt god-like.

QUESTION 2

As with all 10 questions it is recommended that you read the question below, close your eyes, take a few deliberate breaths and reflect on the question. While you breath, see what comes to mind.

There may be several things that come to mind or some vague thoughts. Don't be concerned if you don't have clarity. Just write down whatever emerges.

**What did you want to be as a child?
What did you dream of?**

Once you have made your notes, you may wish to see examples of responses from a few of the Life-Stage subscribers.

Some personal answers to QUESTION 2
"What did you want to be as a child? What did you dream of?"

I dreamt of being a ballet dancer. I'm 63 and still dream of it.

As a child my only dream was to please my parents. Bigger dreams came later.

I wanted to be a doctor - heal people of their mental and physical problems.

This changed regularly, even though I was painfully aware that there were fewer options for girls back then. However, most of the things I dreamt of involved wearing a cape and fighting social injustice!

I wanted to travel around the world and experience as much life as possible.

An actress. and activist. Like Vanessa Redgrave

I knew I was going to be a star baseball player. Oh, until about 12, when I knew I was never going to be a star baseball player!

I wanted to be admired, therefore brilliant, as a concert pianist, like Sparkey in 'Sparkey's Magic Piano'.

Teenager

By thirteen our perception of the world was widening and time was starting to go a faster. We were growing up and big changes were afoot. There was a major growth spurt as our brain sent hormones through the blood stream to different parts of the body. Every one of us went through puberty. What was going on? How much did we understand about the chemicals that were changing our bodies? Our Voices? Our behaviour?

For the last two thousand years there were children and adults. Then, after the Second World War, a new word came over from America. The idea of a 'teenager' seemed alarming to older generations. It conjured up emotional turmoil and rebellion - but this new word 'teenager' was exciting and empowering to many who are now baby-boomers. It gave them an identity and a sense of belonging to something outside the 'boring' adult world.

Before rushing on, the invitation is to stop reading for a moment or two and focus on your breath. Take three deep breaths. And a few more if you wish. They are free! Enjoy the breathing.

By our mid-teens, the education system encouraged us to start specialising in certain subjects. The exam system was part of the shaping of our identity for the adult world to come. Were we going to pursue the arts, the sciences or a trade? For a generation of girls and a few boys there was the 'option' of home economics.

Social Influences

While the zygote cell of our conception contained much of the raw information of wo we are, we have also been shaped by a society that has changed dramatically over the course of our lifetime. The way of life after the second world war bears little resemblance to today. Back in the sixties, life was in analogue with a mass of paper files and limited programming on the television. Computers were still in their infancy and the internet was yet to be invented. Today's baby-boomers witnessed a revolution in the sixties and seventies of ideas, technology, music and fashion that was unprecedented. As we now face the prospect of old age, many of us are now wondering if there is another way to make the most of the second half of life.

Transition

From the sixties onwards, young people were finding their own voice which was frequently used to rebel against the old ways. Many teenagers back then felt they were different from previous generations and there was a sense that *the times they were are a-changing*. In this brave new world, the older generation were often less sure of their role in fostering youth. The old hierarchy was breaking down and many of the established values left over from an Empire were being challenged.

But life in the West was very different from indigenous cultures where the transition from adolescence to adulthood is marked by a rites of passage ceremony. The youth detach from their childhood identity before entering into a sacred or liminal space where they are prepared for their new role as an adult in the community.

For example, teenage boys in the Maasai tribe of East Africa go through a gruelling ordeal before they can be accepted by the community as an adult. The Apache Native Americans held ceremonies for days, with the whole tribe present, to celebrate girls entering their Womanhood. In African culture there is a proverb that youth who are not embraced by the village will burn it down just to feel the heat.

In Western culture there is no such rite of passage and some youth poured their energy into anti-establishment activity.

VANDELISM, is it a world-wide-problem? or just a british problem?

In Venuatu, young men complete their rites of passage by jumping off a rickety, wooden tower.

The end of school or graduation may have been marked by speeches and some drinks, but we had no tribe and there was no formal initiation to support us into this next stage of life. Most of us had to find our own way into adulthood without the support of the tribe and the elders.

QUESTION 3

Before moving into the adult part of the story, there is time to take a few conscious breaths before responding to the question below.

With this question, many thoughts and people might occur to you. The challenge is to focus on just <u>one</u> person. Of course, there is no wrong answer.

Try to remain conscious of your breathing while you let this important person come to the forefront of your mind. Whoever comes to mind now is right person.

It's fine if you want to adapt or change your response at a later date, but the idea is not to create a list. Focus on just one person.

Who did you admire as a teenager?
What values did you admire in them?

Once you have made your notes, you may wish to see examples of responses from a few of the Life-Stage subscribers.

Some Personal answers to QUESTION 3

"Who did you admire as a teenager? What values did you admire in them?"

I admired my music teacher. She was passionate about music and instilled in me a similar love.

Jim Morrison from the Doors. He was wild!!

I admired a leader in the Crusaders who was strong affectionate and caring who seems to be very present with me and was not afraid of wasps.

Violet, a puppeteer. Her independence and creativity.

I admired an ice hockey goal keeper named Glen Hall. He was highly regarded as a gentle person who played with toughness, he showed me a contradiction about being both gentle and tough.

Linda McCartney, for her have-a-go attitude, her photography, for pioneering vegetarian food and being an all-out earth mother. Also for managing to not let her famous hubby and motherhood hold her back.

The person I admired, from aged 8-9 onwards was Scarlett O'Hara - feisty, survive anything, 'fiddle-de-dee' to men who were mesmerised by her, a fighter, an empowered woman in a man's world.

*We don't stop playing because we grow old,
we grow old because we stop playing.*

GEORGE BERNARD SHAW.

Survival & Identity

And so, with or without blessings from the older generation, we entered the adult world – an absurdly complex organism with its arcane institutions and rules. How would we fit in? We had already learnt that the emotional and physical dependency which was acceptable as a child was no longer appropriate. The freedom that we might have had as a child to be curious and playful without inhibition was often curtailed or structured into organised sport or events.

You may have had to cover up your insecurities as a young adult and perhaps you had to 'fake it until you made it' or hide the parts of yourself that didn't fit in with social convention. Vulnerability was seen as a weakness. One way or another you learnt to survive in a complicated environment with its many different compartments. Home life. Work life. Family. Finances.

Friends. We adapted and separated out parts of our personality to survive.

For many of us, this was the prime of life. For some there was the chance to be the first in the family to go to university. Many specialised and defined their field of learning or skills and detached it from the complex web of information that surrounded it. Separation created boundaries for us, and many developed an expertise and competence, so that we could have a quantifiable value in society. And with this came a burgeoning social identity, be it teacher, secretary, electrician, housewife, artist, parent, etc.

Social Backdrop

As a fully-fledged adult, the chances are we were more aware of the events in the outside world than we were as a child. Our vision of the world had broadened and surely some of the dramatic changes in society had come to affect us. Our personal story is bound to be influenced by the social history through which we lived.

Many of the 15 million baby-boomers alive today either witnessed or were part of a social revolution. We saw that the deep-seated conventions and beliefs of the establishment being challenged. By 1969 homosexuality was no longer a crime. Gays and lesbians were starting to find their voice. Three thousand years of patriarchy was being seriously challenged by the women's liberation movement. The contraceptive pill had become available, and sex was coming out from under the covers and into the mainstream. There was excitement and optimism about the future. Many envisioned a society where technology would enable us to be free from the shackles of work. Many felt that things would only get better.

The rapid rise in consumerism was changing many traditional ways of being. Since the second world war the extended family with several generations living under one roof was breaking down. Social wealth brought greater choice and new options. The self-sufficient nuclear family was becoming the norm so children were less likely to witness the day to day lives of their ageing grandparents.

Stereotypes

But whilst some talked of liberation and freedom, others were seeing lucrative marketing opportunities for new products. The "Mad Men" of America had developed increasingly dubious techniques to get us to buy new products and to aspire to a "better life". Idealised stereotypes were portrayed to sell us everything from cigarettes to dishwashers and cars. We were among the first generations to experience such a flood of pervasive advertising which was designed to enter into our subconscious brain.

The reliable father figure was seen as confident and in charge. There was the role model of the caring housewife, while attractive young women were used to sell anything and everything. Images of youth and family were the tools that generated mass consumption. Not surprisingly, it was hard to find positive stereotypes of anyone over fifty. These stereotypes and models of behaviour may well have entered our subconscious adult mind and influenced our choices and our actions.

QUESTION 4

Conscious breathing has many mental and physical healthy benefits, so why not cash in with a few conscious breaths before the responding the next question.

Again, many responses to the question below might occur to you. The idea is to focus on just <u>one</u> challenge. It needn't be the biggest challenge or the most dramatic – just what comes to mind right now.

What one challenge did you face as a younger adult?

Once you have reflected on the question, try to write some words about this challenge.

Some personal answers to QUESTION 4
"What challenge did you face as a younger adult?"

A huge challenge was my relationship to my twin brother who seemed so unhappy and determined to make me do things I didn't want to do.

Finding my personhood within a world that was bigger than I had been prepared for…finding me as an independent human being

Being so much taller than average. Finding shoes and clothes to fit. Being confused with a man.

I was painful shy. I could never ask for what I needed.

Coming from a background that had strong views on what women should be, my main challenges were handling the emotional fall outs when I tried to overcome all the barriers put in my way.

Surviving deep and pervasive shame of being called Fatso.

Bringing up three children as a single parent.

I had to escape the clutches of my overbearing family who wanted to control all of my life choices.

Middle Age

Studies show that the weight of the brain starts to decline by 5% each decade from around the age of 40 due to a reduction in cells.[8] Despite this shrinking, some mental functioning actually improves in middle age. The Seattle Longitudinal Study tracked the cognitive abilities of thousands of adults over 40. The study showed people performed better on tests of verbal abilities, spatial reasoning, maths and abstract reasoning in middle age than they did when they were young adults.

For many their forties were often a time of peak productivity. They had gained expertise in their chosen field and were able to understand problems and find solutions with greater efficiency than their younger colleagues. In the workplace, life experience was seen as a valuable asset and many men (and even a few women) were working their way up the career ladder.

Aspiration

We were one of the first generations to experience the *"you can do anything if you put your mind it"* belief. Social mobility was much talked about, but by midlife, some were becoming more realistic about their

---

[8] Dr. Charles Bernick, Cleveland Clinic Lou Ruvo Center for Brain Health

potential in life and were starting to see the difference between what is possible and what is likely. Some of our youthful dreams and ideals had been tempered by the reality of everyday life – becoming a successful ballet dancer or a professional football player was no longer an option!

We were slowly waking up to the fact that we were no longer young and that one day we would be old. For some there may have been doubt and stress related to one's perceived lack of accomplishment or success in life. Different psychological stress factors came into play as we delt with the subtle changes of growing older.

Dark Night

There is often a point around mid-life that leads to a crisis or a 'dark night of the soul'. It can be triggered by the death of a relative or a friend, being made redundant, divorce or by children leaving home. It may be something small or big that makes people question what lies behind the facade and the labels that they had adopted. What is the point of it all? It is not surprising that many older adults who have survived the full onslaught of the consumerist society, now find there is a lack of fulfilment and meaning in their life. Government statistics show that men in particular find this phase of life to be most challenging.

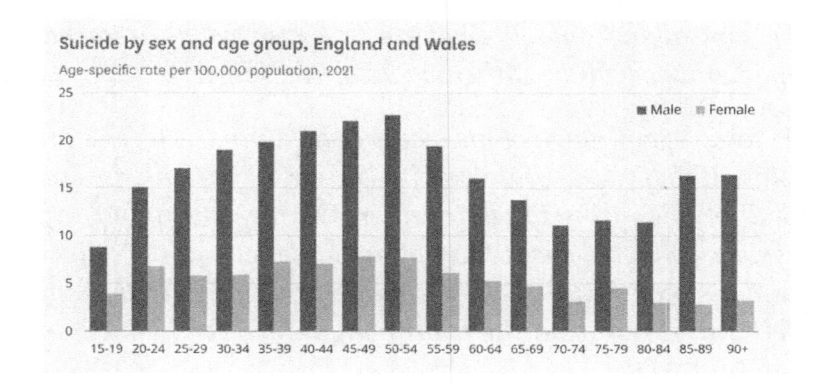

Suicide by sex and age group, England and Wales
Age-specific rate per 100,000 population, 2021

The realisation that the end of your working life may not be far off can bring into question your whole identity. Take Ralph's experience for example;

RALPH'S EXPERIENCE:

For over twenty years, Ralph had taught English Literature at a sixth form college where his positive attitude and charisma were admired by most of his young students. It was the first week of the summer holidays after a hectic end of term when Ralph got a call from his sister.

She told him that their mother was struggling with independent living and they had to start looking at what options there were for her future.

With some resentment Ralph set off in the car to check out one of the care homes a couple of days later. On the journey he kept asking himself what was his responsibility for his mother who had the earlier stages of Alzheimer's.

Having spent much of his working life with lively 17 year olds, Ralph found it disturbing to see all the elderly and frail people eating lunch together. On the return journey, Ralph wondered about the staff redundancies at the college and his own future. By the time he arrived back home, he felt a terror of what the future might hold for him. (to be continued)

All stages of life have challenges but late middle-age can bring up some profound questions about what you're doing with your life and what the future may hold. Again, data shows that late middle-age is the least happy and the most anxious time of life.

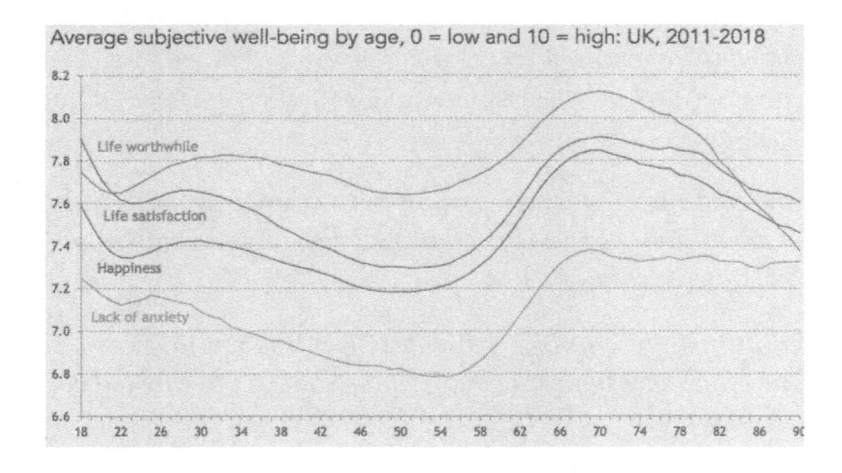

Average subjective well-being by age, 0 = low and 10 = high: UK, 2011-2018

The Menopause

From around forty to fifty-five women usually experienced the menopause which is a natural part of ageing. In some traditional cultures, the end of menstruation is seen as a rite-of-passage from mother to crone[9], but in our culture there was little celebration. Hot flushes and sweats were not only inconvenient, they were the source of embarrassment and even shame especially if the woman was working in an office environment dominated by men. For many women it was a silent transition that brought discomfort and perhaps some sadness that their fertile stage of life was over.

JACKIE'S EXPERIENCE:

Jackie (53) says the heart attack was a blessing. She was an HR manager at a university where there seemed to be a constant series of employment tribunal cases in progress. Some of the disputes had become ugly and the toxic atmosphere became increasingly stressful for Jackie. At home she found her hormonal changes were contributing to stress in her relationship. Her partner longed for the woman Jackie was when they first met twenty years ago.

---

9 The crone is an archetypal figure of the wise woman although the term is often used as an insult

Then one day she collapsed on the pavement four doors up from her house. She was lucky to survive, and the doctor encouraged her to think about all aspects of her lifestyle. Jackie felt some shame about collapsing on the pavement. She had always seen herself as strong and independent. Now she felt she had let herself and everyone else down.

In her recovery time she started to explore how she could change, and one weekend made a very clear intention to 'find her calling' as she put it. It started with watercolours and quickly moved to acrylics before jumping into oils. The canvases became larger and larger and she sold a few of them. Her old peer group thought her artistic journey was eccentric, but she didn't care anymore what people thought. She made new friends and had a couple of exhibitions. She didn't sell much, but she had stopped worrying about the future. After the heart attack, she was living day to day and most days she experienced a sense of freedom and joy that she had not known before her close shave with death.

Before turning to the next page,

do you have time

to stop for a few moments

to treat yourself

to take a few conscious breaths?

It's up to you, of course,

it's your choice.

Everything is up to you.

QUESTION 5

Again, many responses to the question below might occur to you. The idea is to focus on just <u>one</u> achievement or accomplishment. It needn't be the biggest or the most dramatic – just what comes to mind right now.

What one achievement or accomplishment from your adult life comes to mind right now?

Once you have reflected on the question, try to write some words about this achievement.

Some personal responses to QUESTION 5

"What one achievement or accomplishment from your adult life comes to mind right now?"

Travelling around Central and South America for a year. Being self-sufficient.

Bringing up 3 children as a single parent

Becoming a systems network engineer in my mid-30s, having begun a job with a software company as receptionist.

Mentoring young men in the criminal justice system

My family at that time believed that women should be wives and that was it, therefore, not worth educating. My main achievement was to get my 2 degrees and acquire a bunch of other qualifications

Earning my own living. From financial dependence and nil confidence, setting up and building counselling practice, one client at a time

Surviving without being employed by any organisation.

Maintaining a wonderful relationship with my daughter despite many problems.

Separation

The complex world we entered as young independent adults functioned through specialization. Without it there would be no supermarkets and no National Health Service. There would be no sophisticated transport system, and many aspects of our modern world would cease to function.

This segmented view of life is supported by traditional science. The Newtonian or mechanistic approach is sometimes known as reductionism and states that if you want to know how something works, you reduce the system or organism to its most basic form. Then, if you study how each building block of the system behaves independently, you can determine how the whole system works. This sounds logical, and reductionism has produced some extraordinary discoveries such as the atomic structure of matter and the revolution in molecular biology. Many of the developments in psychology, economics and sociology come from studying a phenomenon that is isolated from its context or environment.

Beyond Independence and Separation

Reductionism may be useful up to a point, but viewing ourselves or anything else in life as separate from the environment is ultimately a limited way of looking at the world.

Viewing life only through the lens of independence can cause us great suffering, particularly as we get older. As we will see, the idea that we are independent is a dangerous illusion that can foster isolation in later life.

Are you in a hurry to move on?

Do you have time for three conscious breaths?

Now.

In this precious moment.

The Big Picture

The world of independence gave a limited perspective on life. It provided an illusion of order. It enabled us to function in a results-orientated society. It was a pragmatic mind-set to aid survival in this complex and beguiling culture, but independence is a fragmented and partial view of existence. No one is truly independent.

To view life through the lens of independence is like a small mouse scurrying in the undergrowth of life. The field of vision is small. Everything is in close-up and it's impossible to get a true perspective on what's really going on. It is a fearful existence for there is no knowing what predators are lying in wait. To move into later life with this limited vision will ultimately lead to fearful isolation.

Of course, we have a primal drive to prioritise personal survival, security and comfort, but in the autumn of our days, we come to realise that no matter what we do, and no matter how wealthy or healthy we are, personal survival is not possible. We will die. A growing awareness of death in later life can either diminish us or it can free us to be our true selves.

After middle age, there is a fresh possibility of having a wider vision and seeing beyond the separation of independence. Like an eagle soaring over the landscape, there's a chance to view the whole picture. By consciously ageing, we can develop this vast perspective and find joy, wisdom and courage that we never thought possible in our youth. Beyond separation and division, there is the world of inter-dependence. A world that includes all phenomena, including ageing and death.

Inter-dependence embraces life and death and the true nature of all things. It enables an awareness that life is much greater than just our individual survival. To see life through the lens of inter-dependence is to realise that we are an integral part of the living organism that is planet Earth. It is a holistic point of view where things are viewed in the context of the whole.

Increasingly, scientists are seeing that holism is the reality and that nothing truly exists in isolation[10]. It

---

10 Quarks, for example, combine to form composite particles called hadrons, but it has proved impossible for scientists to view a quark in isolation and in quantum mechanics the mere act of observing an object affects the findings.

is not just a theory from cosmologists and particle physicists. It is a perspective that is having increasing influence in biology, sociology, psychiatry and most branches of science. To understand the essence of a subject, it/he/she needs to be seen in the context of their environment not as an isolated entity. Inter-dependence is the fundamental reality of existence and, if we can embody this perspective in our daily lives, it can lead to inner wellbeing.

As our physical power wanes in the second half of life, there is the possibility to connect with something far greater than our individual self. But we can't access this wonderful state with the mind alone.

Limitations of the Mind

In the independent stage of life, the chances are we will have come to rely heavily on the mind – that logical, thinking part of us that makes judgements and decisions. Accepting that the mind has limitations is absolutely key to development in later life. As we grow older, the meaning of life may become a more urgent question. What's the point of it all? Is there any meaning to existence? To acknowledge that life is a mystery, and that there is much that will remain unknown, is a step towards wisdom. If we can let go of the idea that there is an answer and solution to everything, then we can open up to the joy and wonder of existence.

The mind appears to be nature's most incredible creation as it handles perception, language and memory, but there are some things that the mind is unable to grasp. Our brain contains about 86 billion nerve cells which are connected by trillions of connections, or synapses. Despite such awesome computing power, many scientists[11] suspect that there are aspects of nature and life such as free will and consciousness, that lie outside the limits of human thinking.

The Great Mystery

There are some fundamental mysteries that may never be solved. For example, we don't know how our universe came into being. Particle physicists have a mass of data about what happened a second after the 'big bang', but they don't know what went on a second before. Perhaps the universe has always existed or there are an infinite number of universes. The truth is no one knows, and with every scientific break-through comes more questions. It is in our nature to want answers, so it is hard to accept that there may never be a unifying theory of consciousness or how the cosmos came into being.

---

11 S.J.Blundell: History and Philosophy of Physics Cornell University 2016

The Golden Ration Spiral

However, nature continues to beguile us. For example, fractuals and the golden ratio spiral (there's one of the cover of this book) conform to mathematical formula and exist throughout the natural world. The infinitely complex, repeated patterns are seen in everything from trees, rivers and clouds to sea-shells and seem to indicate an underlying wisdom in the universe.

Fractal are everywhere in nature.

Whether it's cracking DNA coding, doing a sudoku puzzle or working out who did the crime, the human mind loves solving mysteries, but to age consciously and access our inner power as we grow older, there's a need to acknowledge the limitations of the mind.

At the heart of inter-dependence is an acceptance of mystery. This is not to devalue science or rational thought, but being able to abide with not knowing all the answers gives us freedom to fully appreciate life in its wholeness. By going beyond the logical mind-set of independence and we can embracing the unknown and recapture the wonder of the dependent child.

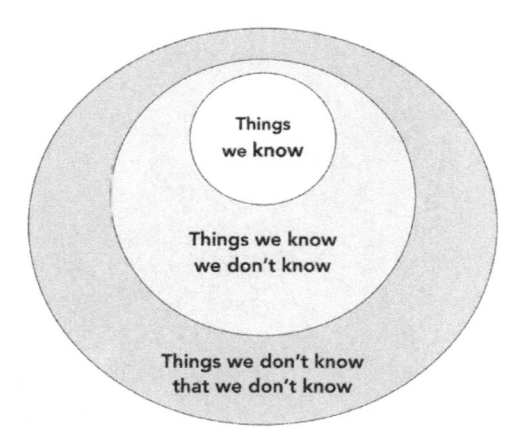

- Things we know
- Things we know we don't know
- Things we don't know that we don't know

Soul or Call It What You Will

Different cultures and traditions use different terminology. For the Lakota tribe in North America, for example, the 'Great Mystery' is not seen as a deity but as an encompassing life force and energy existing in all things. It is a great unifying force that flows in and through all phenomena. Some might refer to the mystery as God while others might call it Qi or fundamental 'life force'. On the Twelve Step programmes, addicts talk about the 'Higher Power'. Whatever we choose to call this energy, it is notoriously hard to define. We can only use the language of our minds which falls short in the face of such a challenge. It is outside of our understanding of time and space. Some may refer to this undefinable energy as simply love.

This might be a judicious place to stop reading for a few moments and to connect to the inhalation and then the exhalation of a few breaths.

The Great Mystery

There's a part of our being which some call the soul that connects to the great mystery. This is the part of us that is not concerned with separation, independence, boundaries, and how much we have in our bank account. It can't make sense of the twenty four hour clock. The soul can't count beyond two. It is not concerned with our individual survival in the mundane world, but it plays a vital part in our moment by moment happiness as we grow older. It is where the deepest joy resides in us. It exists in everyone but while we are in the dependent and independent stage of life, it may well be dormant for much of the time. The soul might put in a strong appearance at the birth of a baby or at the death of a loved one. The soul is undefinable and unqualifiable and is best described by poets such as Rumi, Rainer Maria Rilke or David Whyte. The famous lines below from William Blake's poem, *The Auguries of Innocence,* do not make any logical sense and yet we instinctively know that they contain a deeper truth.

> *To see a World in a Grain of Sand*
> *And a Heaven in a Wild Flower,*
> *Hold Infinity in the palm of your hand*
> *And Eternity in an hour*

Such thought is well outside the realm of profit and loss, but it connects us to the wonder and mystery of life. As the Buddhist philosopher, Daisaku Ikeda said,

Love transcends the individuality of life, and opens our hearts to the true aspect of life which is one and indivisible.

The soul has limitless potential to affect how we are now and right up to and including our death. Our soul is in this breath and our very last. As we grow older our physical energy diminishes and our capabilities may become limited, but we can more than compensate by developing the connection of the soul (or whatever you choose to call it) to the unifying mystery of life.

JACK'S STORY

In 2021, Jack had to cancel the family holiday to Greece due to the Covid epidemic and quarantine regulations. The family went camping instead and on the first night of the trip, Jack couldn't sleep as he lay in the tent worrying about his job.

As it was getting light at 4.30am, Jack got out of his sleeping bag and started to walk from the camp site and down a nearby nature trail. He would be 55 next week and it didn't feel good. He was anxious about his daughters' education. He was uneasy about his marriage. His mum was not well. He was fearful for the future.

As the dawn started to break, Jack followed the path into a wood, not knowing where he was going. He carried on walking for a while until he came to a clearing. He sat on a log feeling empty and alone. He was close to tears as he searched his tired brain for some kind of a solution to his life.

Jack sat there as the morning sunlight started to come through the trees and he became aware of the bird song all around him. After an hour or so, it became obvious to Jack that he was not alone. There was life all around him and despite his problems, the almost-fifty-five-year-old remembered how as a child he had built a camp in the woods with his friend. As Jack slowly walked back to the site, he was full of wonder at the beauty of the morning light on the trees. It felt as though he was re-connecting to something buried deep within him that had been hidden for many years.

Jack's story illustrates how easy it is to be so caught up in survival that we miss the bigger picture. Many feel a sense of loss or emptiness as they come into the second half of life. It's as if something is missing.

Transience and Loss

The world of inter-dependence is not some rose-tinted view of life where cute animals and humans interact harmoniously in a Disneyesque fantasy. It is seeing life for what it truly is. Without illusion. And at times, the world seems harsh and devastatingly cruel.

By the time we get to our fifth decade, most of us will have known plenty of loss. The loss of relatives. The loss of youth and friendships. The loss of dreams. The loss of pets. Even the loss of hair, teeth or 20/20 vision. As we go through the decades, it is inevitable that our losses increase. The mature adult recognises that loss is a part of ageing and a part of life.

There is a Buddhist story about a woman whose baby dies. She is grief stricken and seeks out the Buddha to help her. He tells her to collect a mustard seed from every house where no one has died. The woman sets off but in every house she visits someone has died, and she realises what the Buddha is showing her. Loss is a part of life.

Grief

Grief is the natural response to loss but there is no way to understand grief with the logical mind. There are no easy answers. It is connected to a deeper part of us that some call the soul.

Perhaps with many of our losses, the grief has been covered up. When we were young, we were encouraged to grow out of shedding tears as it showed a vulnerability that was not welcomed. To grieve for something small or to grieve for too long was seen as self-indulgent. In a culture based on independence and materialism, grief is seen as unproductive. It is something that needed to be fixed as quickly as possible. But ignoring our losses does not bode well for our later life.

If we do experience grief, it is generally a private matter unless it's at a funeral. In many indigenous cultures grief is a emotion that is shared with the whole tribe.

It is not ignored or covered up, but is acknowledged in communal ritual and ceremony for the health and well-being of all.

When our grief cannot be spoken, it falls into the shadow and re-arises in us as symptoms. So many of us are depressed, anxious, and lonely. We struggle with addictions and find ourselves moving at a breathless pace, trying to keep up with the machinery of culture. FRANCES WELLER

We do not have to move at a breathless pace. We can stop, if only for a few moments, and become conscious of our breath. Perhaps we are afraid that our grief will overwhelm us, but if we stay conscious of the inhalation and exhalation, we can find a way to connect with the great mystery.

Over the last few decades, ideas around communal grief practices have started to take root in the West. The story of Helen who attended one such ritual is an example of how important acknowledging grief can be;

HELEN'S EPERIENCE

Some would say that Helen lived a very privileged life. She was active in her community, though was seen as a little detached and aloof. On a well-being retreat at the age of 58, she was invited to participate in something that people referred to as a 'grief circle'. At first Helen thought this a

strange idea. No one close to her had died recently. She was generally happy with her life and grief was not something she wished to be involved with. But she went along with her friend.

There were around a dozen participants in a circle near an old oak tree in the woods. The facilitator invited them to step in and form an inner circle if they had a parent who had died. She watched from the outer circle as some on the inner circle named their dead parents. Helen felt awkward watching these people open up to their grief. When the facilitator invited anyone in the outer circle who had a close friend die, Helen stayed where she was. And then it hit her; one of her best friends, Elise, had drowned in Greece when she was on holiday with her parents. But that was when they were both teenagers. Helen stepped into the inner circle and spoke her friend's name for the first time in over thirty years. She thought she had dealt with her emotions around this tragedy but under the huge oak tree she felt the grief coming in waves to the surface. She felt safe enough to allow her feelings to emerge completely as she started sobbing. And then her grief seemed to embrace the pain and loss of so much more than just her friend.

When Helen had finished weeping her tears, she felt exhausted but also a wonderful sense of freedom and peace came over her. She started to wonder about all the grief people had buried in their hearts and never let go of. That evening around a camp fire, Helen found herself laughing in way that she hadn't since she was a teenager. This episode had a powerful effect on the next stage of Helen's life.

Grief & Joy

It is not possible to realise our full potential if we are hiding our grief. If we supress the grief, we cannot fully experience the joy of living and so we live in what Frances Weller calls *a flat-line culture* where we are unable to fully experience grief, joy and life in its fullness.

If you are fully conscious of your inter-dependence, it is natural to experience the depths of your grief but also the wonder and joy of life. From an inter-dependent perspective both grief and joy are deeply connected. Relationships are given power and depth because consciously or unconsciously we know they are finite. The joy that comes from a beautiful connection with another living being, deepens our grief when we lose that relationship.

As we grow older there is the possibility to feel joy and unconditional happiness despite our many losses and connect to something much larger than our small, independent selves. In the second half of life, the opportunity to access our full potential through a connection with the great mystery lies in the acceptance of loss and the transience of life. (There is more about grief under the notes at the back of the book.)

QUESTION 6

As with all the questions, take 3 conscious breaths and relax the shoulders. If you enjoyed the breaths, why not take a few more.

This next question may bring up some uncomfortable emotions. If you need to skip this question and come back to it later, please do. The idea is to focus on just <u>one </u>loss. It needn't be the biggest – just what comes to mind right now.

It can be the loss of anything or anyone. Perhaps a piece of jewellery you lost, or a pet that died when you were young.

Keep taking conscious breaths. And when you bring one loss to the centre of your mind, try not to have an judgements about the loss. Whether it is a large loss or a small one, it doesn't matter. Try and stay with your feelings around this one loss. Then take three strong, conscious breaths before answering the question

What one loss have you experienced in your life?

Once you have reflected on the question, try to write some words about the loss.

Some personal responses to QUESTION 6
"What one loss have you experienced in your life?"

I have lost both my parents without witnessing their deaths.

Though I didn't know the depth of the loss at the time, my grandfather's death left a huge hole that is only now being truly honoured.

Losing my younger brother , my only sibling, when he died of lung cancer in his sixties..

The death (or killing) of our first dog. I remember the last time we walked him before having him put to sleep. It was excruciating (I suspect for both him and us) and I held him as the vet injected him to death. Sad is not a word that applies. Soul-destroying!

My sexual power/nature, learning very young it wasn't safe to live energetically as a sensual let alone sexual being.

My business partner died and I had no closure. No good bye. No funeral. We didn't always get on. But I miss him.

My chocolate standard poodle over 35 years ago as he was so attached to me he was jealous of my baby son, so for my son's protection I had to find a new home for Joe who was only 6 years old.

Integration

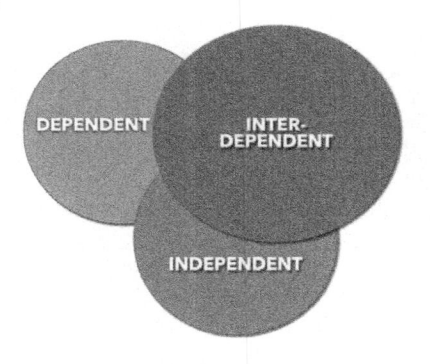

In reality, the three stages of dependent, independent and inter-dependent are not rigid and linear. From an inter-dependent perspective, we can freely embrace the dependent child or the aspiring independent adult within us. There is no need to reject any aspect of life. There are times when we are dependent and times when we require an independent frame of mind, but as we grow older, there is great benefit and freedom in consciously expanding our vision to the big picture.

Causality

You do not have to be old to see that all life is inter-dependent. It is now well documented how the rampant exploitation of the earth and human greed has had a knock-on effect on the health of the oceans, the forests, animal and plant life. All aspects of our planet are inter-connected and people of all ages are waking up to the realisation that life is inter-dependence. Many despair. They think it is too late. Many think that their actions will make little difference. Many understand inter-dependence theoretically, but would be unwilling to change their own actions.

The key question for us mature adults is how can we embody an inter-dependent spirit and reveal our full potential for the benefit of ourselves and for others. How can we develop that part of us that sees the bigger picture? How can we see something greater than our own personal salvation. Even in our dotage, could we model behaviour that gives hopes to younger generations?

In the next section of this book, we focus on the what kind of intention might best serve you now and in the future. But before then, we need to look at what might prevent you from reaching your full potential as an adult.

Arrested Development

We have survived a few decades now and have probably developed some effective coping mechanisms to deal with fear, but for most of us there is an underlying angst about our own future and the future of humanity. On a personal level, we may worry about losing physical or mental capacity, losing friends or relatives or not having enough resources in our old age. And then, there's the question of how we will be at the moment of our death. To the independently-minded individual, death might be seen as a failure of the body and a tragic defeat in the ego's long effort to survive.

The Fear of Death

From an inter-dependent perspective, ageing and death are part of a bigger picture. They are an essential process which enables new life to come into existence.

Without the death of bacteria, microbes, plants, trees, insects, birds, fish, mammals and especially humans, the planet would be overrun with life. Without death, all life on earth would cease to function within a few days.

It is easy for us to believe that we are somehow separate from this natural law of the universe (what physicists call the second law of thermodynamics) because we have consciousness, but this disconnection from nature greatly magnifies our fears and limits our life potential as we grow older.

In today's secular world, the reality of death is pushed to the very edge of our collective consciousness, so that we don't have to think about it. With the decline of the extended family, old age and death are frequently taken care of by poorly paid professionals. Family and friends of the sick and dying do not need to be involved in the end of life process. Such alienation from the reality of life increases the fear of old age and death as it filters down through the generations and into our communities.

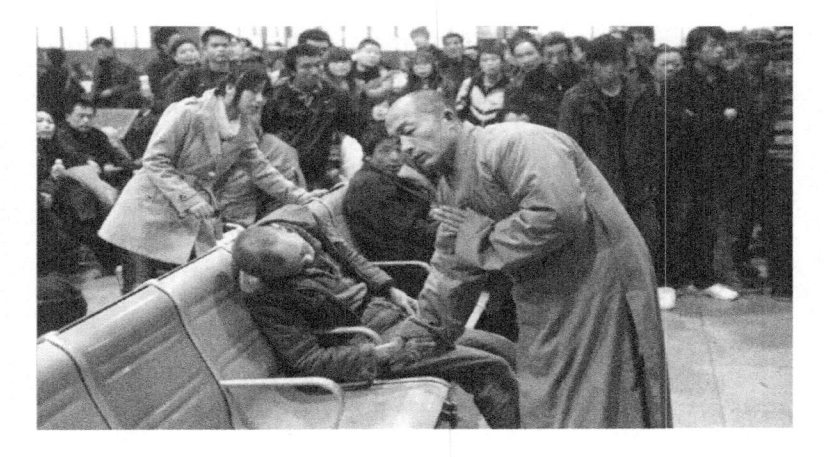

In a busy train station in China a passing monk says prayers for a man who has died.

In a culture devoted to materialistic wellbeing, it is morbid to think about death. To talk about the end of life in polite society is considered taboo. Distractions and the media can prevent us from looking at our fears, but ignoring them makes the fear more powerful.

Hitchcock and other directors of horror movies were aware that fear is most potent when it is unseen. A few threatening hints and some edgy music and the human imagination fills in the gory details which are more terrifying that any mise-en-scène could conjure up.

Often our fears for the future inter-twine on a subliminal level. Whether it is tyrannical leadership, a killer virus, invasive technology or global warming, there is no shortage of social concerns that combine with our personal fears to create a bleak and terrifying future. But we do not need to be a victim of fear. We can with conscious breathing and clear intention use the fear to open up to our greater self.

(There is more about how we can come to terms with out mortality in the notes at the back of the book.)

Reptilian Brain

The need for life and the fear of death are hard-wired into us. The function of the reptilian part of our brain is to keep us alive. It controls our vital functions such as reflexive behaviours, heart rate, breathing and body temperature. In earlier years our fears might have protected us from foolish impetuosity. In later life, fear can be a destructive force if it is given free reign. It can prevent us from being who we truly are. In the face of mortality, the independently-minded individual develops one of the fight, flight or freeze responses to the threat of old age and death.

The Fight Response

The fight response is about doing all that we can to overcome the physical and mental aspects of ageing. It involves staying youthful-looking and active for as long as possible. This often referred to as the positive ageing movement which sounds wonderful, but there is a shadow side. Social media has helped a bandwagon of anti-ageing gurus promote products and services designed to keep us looking and feeling younger. In the era of the selfie, looking good is closely associated with feeling good. The positive ageing movement is thriving and appealing to baby-boomers to 'live life to the full'. Magazines that target an older readership use images of younger-looking models who are "ageing successfully".

Advertisers hint at a happy and affluent lifestyle for older generations. There is the smiling and kind grandparent with children on their knee, or the distinguished mentor figure dispensing wisdom. A woman surfing in her 80s is held up as an inspiring role model. The message is that that we, too, can achieve incredible things if we try hard enough. Some might be encouraged - *if they can do it, so can I*! But for those who are struggling with the ageing process, it is unhelpful. The spirit and courage that leads to such brave endeavours may be admirable, but there may also be a lack of wisdom and compassion. There is often a competitive element to such achievements that boosts the ego of the individual.

Of course, we want to be making the most of our lives. Who wants to be asleep in an armchair when you could be out catching some big waves? Or shuffling around a potting shed when you could be running marathons? Avoiding such stereotypes of ageing can be a seductive message for those of us in the second half of life, but it can also put a pressure on us to perform and keep up appearances. We are getting a barrage of images and messages that tell us that getting old is negative and death is a failure.

Yes, of course, we want to stay fit and active for as long as we can, but our well-being in the second half of life is much more complex than staying fit and active. Ageing well is not so much about accomplishments and running marathons although the positive ageing adverts would like us to think so. We can't access our inner power if we are over-concerned with superficial looks and achievements. If we are pre-occupied with appearances and a bucket list of things to achieve, we miss the opportunity to connect with our greater self.

In the face of ageing and death, the fighter wants to *live life to the full* while they still can. This spirit appears admirable and sometimes heroic but the fight response can lead to materialistic hedonism that involves *getting the most out of life* - no matter the cost to others or to the planet. This maybe the cry of the addict and the compulsive pleasure-seeker. If your retirement plan is to lie on the beach drinking cocktails, you may find there is a down side. The fight response is generally seen as a positive quality in our culture, but it can lead to denial and separation.

The Flight Response

The flight response stems from the belief that some people have that they will not die or that death is not the end. This is common and understandable in young people who hope that science will have sorted out the small problem of ageing and death by the time that they grow old.

Some billionaires who want never to be separated from their vast wealth, have sunk huge sums into scientific and pharmaceutical companies so they can develop solutions for longevity and immortality. It's a booming business, but re-coding DNA or implanting nano-technology is more likely to lead to eternal isolation and misery than to happiness.

The idea of cybernetic immortality where peoples' biological body parts are replaced with indestructible artificial equivalents is the product of reductionist thinking – the terrifying dangers of which have been exploited by numerous science fiction writers.

The Freeze Response

The freeze response is a numbing of our natural energy and emotions and places emphasis on safety and security. This primitive response is based on the idea that if you keep yourself small and inactive, the predator will not notice you. As we grow older, there are many pressures on us to stay timid and keep our lives small. The tendency is to hang on more tightly to what we've got and to what we know rather than embrace the larger vision.

It seems natural that people become more safety and security conscious as they grow older but this can lead to a half-life existence. Take the story of Grace's aunt, for instance;

GRACE'S STORY:

In her twenties Grace moved to London and was asked by her mother to visit an ageing relative who lived in a wealthy suburb of the city. She'd never met her great aunt before, but bought some fruit and chocolate as an offering.

When she entered the big house, it was almost dark and Grace could hardly see her aged relative, so she went to turn the light on. Immediately the aunt snapped at her to turn it off. 'I haven't got money to burn on electricity,' were the old woman's exact words. Grace listened to her great aunt's complaints for a while, but didn't stay long. Two years later, the woman died leaving her two million pound inheritance to a cat's home.

Like many elderly people, Grace's aunt had frozen her emotions and responses to life.

The Neocortex

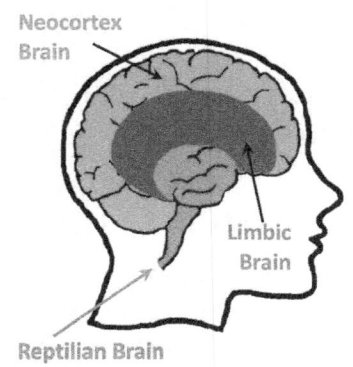

While the reptilian brain has an essential function in keeping you alive, there are other parts of your brain that have developed over millions of years of evolution. The most recent of these is the neocortex that manages sensory perception, emotion, and cognition.

Your neocortex is the part of your brain that allows you to read and, hopefully process this book. It also has the ability to moderate the effects of the reptilian response, so that you need not be enslaved to your most primitive reactions all of the time.

While some people think of fear as an *'intensely unpleasant emotion'* (Wikipedia), others pay good money to put themselves in dangerous and frightening situations. Whether it's bungee jumping or watching horror movies, there's no shortage of customers when it comes to fear. Dangerous pursuits such as mountaineering or diving off high cliffs might seem foolish, but fear can trigger adrenaline that increases energy and a sense of being fully alive. Take this experience from Sabrina for example;

SABRINA'S EXPERIENCE

Jack was proud of his daughter's achievements. At forty-four Sabina had a successful accounting business with her partner and had just acquired one of the hottest digital media companies as a new client.

But Jack was not so happy about his daughter's sporting activities. She had been surfing for a while, but when Sabina went chasing some extreme waves in Portugal, Jack felt she was being irresponsible. She had two teenage children, and he asked his daughter to reconsider her trip. It was a dangerous activity. What if something happened to her? It was typical of Sabina to respond to her father's question with detailed research. She wrote down her directives for the end of her life and what her wishes were, should she no longer have mental capacity. She was very clear about what she did and didn't want to happen. She detailed all of the arrangements for her own funeral including the type of coffin and the songs she wanted playing. And then she re-drafted her will. It took her a few days but she felt somehow liberated. Jack asked his daughter if she had a death wish. 'No', said Sabrina. 'But I'm going to die sometime and I'm not going to live in fear.' [12]

Risk Adverse

It is not necessary to go extreme surfing in later life to feel fully alive, but prioritising security and comfort above everything else doesn't lead to wellbeing. There is a tendency as we age to hang on more tightly to what we've got and what we know, rather than embrace a larger vision. Generally, it seems as though the older people become, the more they look for the safest option. This might seem eminently sensible, but without awareness, we can 'freeze' our life and limit our inner power and potential.

The fear of ageing and death is natural, but there is no need to respond from the reptilian brain. There is no need to catastrophise and assume the worst. When the fear arises we can breathe into it. Consciously taking some air into the lungs and observing the fear helps moderate the fight, flight or freeze response. The more that we practice using the breath in this way, the more we can transform some of the challenges of ageing.

---

12 Planning for the end of life is a process that has practical, emotional and psychological benefits. You'll find a brief guide at the back of the book.

Humans inhale and exhale throughout their life, but to stay conscious of the breath in times of stress can change the narrative around growing older. It is simple and it costs nothing. As we will see in the next section of the book, when the tool of conscious breathing is combined with a clear life intention, we can unlock some of the treasures hidden within us.

QUESTION 7

Time for a few conscious breaths and clear your mind for a moment before considering the next question.

Bring to mind one thing that you are afraid of. It need not be the biggest or most terrifying fear.

If you feel unsafe or overwhelmed by the question, please move on to the next page.

Whether imagined or real; whether big or small, focus on whatever fear comes to mind right now.

Keep the breathing as steadily as you can.

What one fear that comes to mind right now?

Once you have reflected on the question, try to write some words down in your journal

Some personal responses to QUESTION 7

"What one fear that comes to mind right now?"

Becoming blind

My fear of heights is so strong that if I see a picture of someone climbing a dangerous rock face, I feel physically unsafe.

Terrified of rats. And snakes. And probably most creepy crawlies.

Loss of physical or mental competence as I age.

I fear leaving the gas on. I have to keep checking that it is off even though I have just checked it.

My fear is I'll make mistakes in life-choices - eg marriage, to stay or go; spending money.

Pain. Excruciating pain.

The fear of my partner dying before me is terrifying.

Dementia. I so fear losing my memory. My memory is fading and letting me down now. Is it due to age or something worse? The thought of dementia really frightens me.

My fear biggest fear is loneliness and feeling cut off from the world.

PART 2

LIFE INTENTION

*Genius can be bound in a nutshell
and yet embrace the whole fullness of life.*

THOMAS MANN

Why an Intention?

In later life, the future is especially uncertain. If you are wealthy, you might be able to plan materially for later life, so you have all the support mechanisms in place, but how do you prepare mentally, emotionally or spiritually?

For thousands of years religious communities have offered belief systems to support wellbeing in later life. Older members of a congregation might gain comfort through faith and guidance from the priest, rabbi and imam, whereas, today we live in a mostly secular world where around 50% of us have no affiliation to a religious community.

With the decline of the extended family and a lack of elder role models, many turn to the internet for help in coming to terms with growing older. Within the many trillions of words about ageing on the internet[13], you will find thousands of blogs, podcasts, videos, aphorisms and affirmations on ageing. Amidst all the advertisements for anti-ageing products, they may find useful information or if you are lucky, some wise

---

13 In the Google search bar, 'aging', the American spelling, offers up 1,620,000,000 results.
'Ageing', the UK spelling offers up 305,000,000

voices. You may discover affirmations that resonates with you such as;

Don't be afraid of death, be afraid of an unfulfilled life.

One day you'll be just a memory for some people. Do your best to be a good one.

While there is useful information about ageing on the internet, it is ease to end up swamped and confused.

Internal Clarity.

In the Life-Stage Community, the focus is on exploring what it is that you want for your life now, and as you grow older. It is about making a profound choice and commitment. The process in this section of the book is about finding how you want to be … rather than what you want to do. It is about being fully conscious of the qualities that are most important to you and how to realise them now and for the rest of your days. By consciously breathing with a clear intention, it is possible to transform fears about ageing into connection and purpose. It may take some effort to get clarity about intention, but once you have made a distinct choice, the process simply requires a few minutes of your time every day. With commitment and consistency you can access your greater self no matter what age you are.

Definition

You have probably spent much of your life in an environment where goals and targets have been an important factor in daily life, so before continuing, let's be clear about what a life intention is and put it into some context.

NEW YEARS RESOLUTION

Often a guilt response and an attempt to change what you judge to be a negative behaviour.

Eg. *I'm going to go on a diet and exercise everyday*

SHORT-TERM GOAL / TARGETS

Something to be accomplished within a specific time frame. A clearly defined goal is a powerful way to get what we need and/or to measure progress.

Eg. *My goal is to sort out all my tax affairs by the end of the month.*

INTENTION / DETERMINATION / PURPOSE

Setting a wider resolution for your health, relationship, life style, career, etc

Eg. *My intention is to find the right partner to share my life with.*

LIFE INTENTION

A life intention is generally the result of a personal exploration to find your soul's deepest desire for the rest of your life. It serves as a guide and reminder of what is important to you on the most profound level. In moments of confusion or doubt, it can provide focus and clarity. It can create healthy boundaries and gives a profound sense of freedom and joy.

Eg. *My life intention is to be wise and courageous in order to bring healing and joy to myself and others.*

The Law of Attraction

The 'law of attraction' is a results-orientated phenomenon with a foundation in positive psychology, goal-achieving research, and mind-brain sciences. It states that like tends to attract like and positivity usually attracts positivity, and negativity usually attracts negativity.

Such books as *The Secret* by Rhonda Byrne have spawned an industry of self-help manuals which focus mainly on the materialistic or achievement aspects of the law of attraction. If we want money, for example, we have to believe we can get it. This belief will then work into our thoughts which will transfer into words so that we take the action to get the money we desire. The law of attraction is not a new idea nor is it a secret. Over 2,500 years ago the Chinese philosopher, Lao Tzu wrote;

Watch your thoughts, they become your words;
watch your words, they become your actions;
watch your actions, they become your habits;
watch your habits, they become your character;
watch your character, it becomes your destiny.

Many of the self-help courses based on the law of attraction are aimed at an audience who aspire to be rich, powerful or charismatic. The gurus of the law of attraction talk about how the universe provides for you if you make a clear intention. This may be true but the law of attraction is even stronger if the connection with the universe is a two-way, inter-dependent relationship.

In other words, when we have a 'life intention' that is about giving as well as receiving, we access greater power. So, we need to be clear and conscious about what we want for ourselves and others. The universal forces are unlikely to support you if you are vague, confused or inconsistent.

Past, Present and Future

This present moment contains both our past and the future

The sentence above may sound fantastical or meaningless to you, so we're going to start by looking at how our past is contained in the present.

But first, it may be beneficial to stop reading for just a few moments and take three deep, precious breaths.

We have come a long way from the single cell zygote. We arrive in the present with a long history. We are a rich mix of genetic and environmental influences. The dependent stage of life will have shaped much of our personality and behaviours. There have been decades of learning, adapting and finding ways to meet emotional and physical needs.

Whatever you have experienced is contained within this present moment. If you stop to breath consciously, you may get a sense of the past within you. All the tiny, long-forgotten incidents are there in your life. Moments of joy. Of excitement. Of pain and of boredom. You may have developed coping mechanisms to alleviate the suffering, but it is all part of who you are now. So how can we adapt and change when we have so much history? By middle-life, habits and behaviours are well established. We are rooted in own personality. The story of our past is etched deep into our being. The neurological pathways are well trodden and as time goes by, it can feel as though meaningful change becomes more difficult. Changing the patterns can seem as though we are standing on a table while trying to lift the table. It seems impossible.

Letting Go

Most of us in the second half of life find it difficult to let go of the past and move into the next stage of life. The experiences and memories are the story of our lives. Whether good or bad, many in the afternoon of life cling onto their stories and identities. The attachment to past can be physical, mental and emotional. It is quite common in the UK for people around retirement age to down-size their house as they get older and this can be challenging on all levels as Sarah found out;

SARAH'S EXPERIENCE

After her partner had died at the age of 56, Sarah was left alone in the three bedroom house in which she had brought up her two children. A year after the funeral she decided that the time had come to try and move on from the past.

She contacted an estate agent and started to look at the logistics of downsizing. The whole process was surprisingly easy until she had to decide what she would and wouldn't take to her new two bedroom apartment in a retirement village.

Sarah had never thought of herself as a hoarder, but she had accumulated cupboards and drawers full of possessions over the decades. She started in the spare room which was mostly full of old clothes and books, but she made painfully slow progress. There was a green scarf given to her by an aunt. She didn't like the scarf and she didn't like the aunt, but she still agonised over putting it into the 'to-go' pile. Sarah felt overwhelmed with emotion and the task ahead of her.

Sarah's predicament is common in many stages of life but it can be particularly difficult as we leave youth and middle age behind. It is not just possessions. We carry around a vast archive in our minds of thoughts, opinions, judgements and ideas that have been within us for decades. Some may be useful, but many will not serve us now or at any time in the future.

Of course, it's not possible to delete these thoughts and memories as though they were computer files that can be dropped into the trash, but there comes a time when it is useful to review our life and re-appraise what is important to us now.

Evolving

If we are to thrive in the second half of life, we need to consciously evolve. We do not have to continue with the fossilised versions of who we were in mid-life. It is worth noting a statement often attributed to Charles Darwin;

It is not the strongest of the species that survives, nor the most intelligent that survives. It is the one that is most adaptable to change.

Through breathing with a clear intention, it is possible to integrate the past without analysing or rejecting any part of what we've experienced since our manifestation as a zygote. Whatever our story and regardless of the wounds we have suffered, we do not have to be a victim. There is no escaping the past but there is no need to be limited by former experiences. There is no need to fix anything for a life intention to bring you in contact with your greater self.

Catalyst for Change

Retirement seems like a natural time to review your life. If you have spent the better (or worse) part of your adult life in a work environment, you would do well to consider how you want to live now. But there are other events, that can be a catalyst for change in later life. In the case of Bettina, it was an empty nest and the death of her father.

BETTINA'S EXPERIENCE

When she was seven, her daughter used to ask her mother about her childhood, but Bettina never wanted to talk about her upbringing. Bettina's past was a closed book. There was little family connection of any type other than the occasional birthday card. As time passed, Bettina saw her teenage daughter becoming more engaged in her own life until she only came back to the flat to eat and sleep.

When Bettina heard that her estranged father was in a hospice, she went to visit him not because of love or duty but out of a sense of curiosity. She couldn't imagine her father being vulnerable, so despite some trepidation, she went to the hospice to see him. The best she could say about her Father was that he was a cold man.

He did recognize her but didn't say anything and then fell asleep. She sat there by his bedside with the staff going about their business. A doctor told her about her father's diagnosis but Bettina didn't take any of the information in. She felt numb. She sat for a long time by his bedside while all around her was a sense of calm in the hospice. Before the visiting hours were up, one of the volunteers who was a woman of her own age made a cup of tea for Bettina.

One evening about six months after her father died, Bettina was on her second glass of wine when she felt something approaching disgust at her life which gave rise to an inner resolve for change. She kept thinking about her time at the hospice and the woman who made her a cup of tea.

The next day Bettina didn't go to the council offices where she worked, but went to the hospice to find out how she could become a volunteer. She felt that this would be a good place to start a new life.

The death of Bettina's father and the compassion of the volunteer helped her move on from the old story of her individual self.

Like a river, life never flows backwards. We can't change or fix the past. We are where we are, and we can only go forward. As we will see, the way to integrate our past with present moment is to consciously breath with a clear intention for our whole life.

The Future in the Present

Perhaps part of the reason, we don't want to let go of the past is because of our fear of the unknown future. No matter how much we try to live in the present moment, it is human nature to speculate. There are plenty of *what if* questions that may emerge as we grow older.

> *What if my partner dies before me?*
>
> *What if the pain in my hip gets any worse?*
>
> *What if my money runs out?*
>
> *What if I become isolated and lonely?*

The fears may prompt some practical action such as booking an appointment with the doctor or making a will. But if the fear lurks in the depths of our being - it will ultimately narrow our vision and erode our life force. It is disempowering to dwell too long on such tragic possibilities that the mind might conjure up.

So, the invitation is to take three deep breaths. When you become aware of your breath, there's a possibility to move past the separate, independent self and connect with your true nature. For all of us conscious beings, there are only two absolute certainties in life.

YOUR PRESENT BREATH
&
YOUR FINAL BREATH

Anything outside these two moments is speculation. Tomorrow may or may not happen. Rather than fearing death and pushing it away, with a clear intention we can start to integrate it into the reality of the present moment. Talking and thinking about death will not kill us but can greatly enrich our lives. Awareness of mortality is the source of our inner power in later life. The inter-dependent mature adult can abide with the not knowing. Once we accept that quality of life is more important than quantity, we will be freeing ourselves from the burden of fear and moving towards unlocking our inner treasure.

(There is more information about engaging with mortality in the notes section at the back of the book.)

The next question is important in getting clarity about what you want for your life. Answering the question fully may feel like letting go of a heavy rucksack that has been carried for many years. It may take longer to answer than the previous questions, so don't rush it. Find a quiet space without distractions. Give yourself at least 15 minutes. If you struggle with the question or feel uncomfortable answering it, move onto the next section.

QUESTION 8

It starts as always with where you are now. Sitting, standing, lying, kneeling. However you are in the present moment. Aware of any sounds around you…your body's contact with the floor or the chair. And your breath… Inhaling … Exhaling. Each breath will lead to the next breath and to the next and to the next… …until eventually you will reach your final breath. It may be months, years or decades away. You don't know. And right now, that is not important.

Keep breathing in the present moment. Breath it in. And visualise how you would like to die. Imagine that you can die in exactly the way that you want. How would it be? In a room? On a bed? What are the sheets and the pillow-cases made of? Who is with you? Or are you alone? What kind of day is it outside. Is a window open?

Or perhaps you would rather die in nature. Under a tree by a river? The choice is yours. Is there music being played as you take your last breath? What sounds can you hear? A human voice or the birds singing? This is your big, and final moment in this life. It will most definitely come. How would you like it to be?

Continues…

> **QUESTION 8 (continued)**
>
> **How would you like to be as you take your last breath?**
>
> Stay conscious of your breathing in the present moment and think how you would like to feel at the end of your life. How could you describe this feeling in words? Imagine your ideal death in as much detail as possible and write detailed notes about it.
>
> If you struggle with the question or feel uncomfortable answering it, move onto the next section.

MIRANDA'S EXPERIENCE

After a successful career in business, Miranda retired at the age of 58 to spend more time with her father who was suffering from Alzheimer's. Previously, Miranda had been labelled a 'captain of industry', but now she felt alone and lost as she tried to comfort her father in the early hours of the morning.

In her work life she had been involved in formulating values and mission statements for fledgling companies to get funding. Now Miranda began to wonder what the vision was for her own future. How would later life be for her?

As her father lost more mental capacity, Miranda started to clarify what it was she wanted for herself and how she wanted to be. She knew she would require all her strength to support herself and her family through the coming months and years.

The process was more difficult than creating a company mission statement, but after some trial and error, Miranda formulated a clear statement of intent for her life and memorised it.

There were many difficult situations within the family as her father's condition worsened, but Miranda felt that her life intention kept her strong through the darkest of times.

Finding the Seed of Intention

We're going to explore how to find the seed of your life-intention and we'll suggest a method for using your life-intention as a means to transform concerns about ageing into connection and purpose.

Knowing what you want for your life on the deepest level is not easy. You may have many ideas about what you don't want – loss of physical or mental capacity for example. But what precisely do you want? It can be tricky deciding on what film to watch from the extensive menu on a streaming channel. However, choosing how you want to be for the rest of your life is more challenging. Don't worry, the next few pages will take you through a process that will help you get clarity. You may have some hazy thoughts about how you would like it to be, but it is only when you are crystal clear about your soul's desire for the rest of your life that you can realise your full potential.

Inner Critic

Just before we get started on finding the seed of intention, we need to address an important part of you that may want to have a say in this process.

Throughout your long life, you have relied on the 'inner critic' to help choose your path and to keep you safe. In the autumn of your days, there may be a natural tendency to be more cautious, but beware of the part of you that wants to keep everything as safe as possible. While respecting this rational part of your brain, try to stay open to the possibility of finding undiscovered resources and treasure in your life.

The statement below is a bold claim:

> *A life-intention is a powerful tool to transform the fear of ageing into meaning and purpose.*

This is a hypothesis that needs to be thoroughly questioned and tested before we can say it has any validity. If you accept such a statement at face value, you may not get the most from this process. On the other hand, if you dismiss it as just hype, then you may miss this opportunity to access inner resources you didn't know you had.

A strong life-intention should be stress-tested again and again, so that it is a tool that you can come to rely on. As you will discover, it is very much a personal experience, so regardless of whether it works for others, you need to prove that it works for yourself, otherwise a life intention is meaningless.

While working on a life-intention, you may find that this inner critic has much to say. This voice inside your head may find all kinds of objections to you engaging fully with this process. The voice may say something like;

INNER CRITIC: *You can't teach an old dog new tricks.*

This may be true, but you're not a dog. Dogs don't have a highly developed cerebral cortex. You do not have to be ruled by the reptilian part of your brain.

INNER CRITIC: *This won't work for me.*

It certainly won't work if you are committed to that belief.

INNER CRITIC: *I don't need an intention for my life. I can rely on my own common sense.*

You and your environment are changing all the time. The Laboratory of Neuro Imaging at the University of Southern California estimates we have around 70,000 thoughts each day which is why it is useful to define our deepest need. Whatever distractions might occur, you can get back in alignment with what it is you really want for your life.

INNER CRITIC: *What distractions are you on about?*

Shopping. Sport. Box sets. News. Social media. There's no shortage of distractions. It is increasingly difficult to avoid them.

INNER CRITIC: *Summing up what I want for my life in a few words is too simplistic. I'm much more complex than that.*

Yes, you are extremely complex, but after so many decades of living in this complex world, a mental de-cluttering can free you up to access your inner potential.

INNER CRITIC *I've spend much of my adult life having goals and targets. Now I've retired I just want to put my feet up and take it easy.*

Fine, but without clarity, it is easy to drift into later life without motivation or direction.

Breakdown of a Life Intention

There are no rules about making a life intention but it is useful to include some or all of the following criteria.

SELF

Does your life intention capture the essence of how you aspire to be in the world?

OTHERS

Does your life intention capture the essence of how you aspire to connect with others?

RESILENT

Can your life intention serve you in all circumstances, both now and right up to the end of your life?

TRANSFORMATIVE

Could your life intention transform concerns about growing older into meaningful connection and purpose?

MEMORABLE

Is your life intention easy to remember? Are the words pleasing to you?

An Example Of A Life Intention

As a mature adult, you can embody the inter-dependent nature of all life by choosing an intention that works for you as well as for other people. Below is an example of what a life intention might look like;

The intention for my life is to be courageous and wise in order to bring healing and joy to myself and others.

This example encapsulates some key qualities that were prized by Indian, Chinese and ancient Greek philosophers. The qualities of courage, wisdom and compassion are as relevant today as they were in the time of Shakyamuni Buddha or Socrates. An intention for such things might be useful in any stage of life but it is particularly appropriate to people in the second half of life who want to fulfil their potential.

Of course, you can create your own life intention or you can adapt the statement given above, but the next few pages, will explain why this form of words holds power.

COURAGE

*The intention for my life is to be (**courageous**)...*

It is natural to be fearful around ageing and the end of life. Fortunately, it is possible to transform this fear with an intention to manifest your innate courage.

INNER CRITIC *I don't do courage. I'm terrified of pain.*

This is not just about physical courage. There's mental and emotional courage. Sometimes it takes courage just to keep going and not give up in the face of adversity. It's an inner strength that can help you maintain a sense of purpose, especially when confronted with great difficulties.

INNER CRITIC *You've either got courage or you haven't. I don't think I have it.*

That's why you need the intention. It's inevitable that there will be difficulties as we grow older. Courage is essential if you want to age well. Fortunately, it's a quality that you can develop.

INNER CRITIC *It might work for some, but I don't think I'll ever be courageous.*

You will never know your own strength unless you plant the intention for courage in your life.

INNER CRITIC *Just talking about courage brings up a fear of my own lack of courage.*

You have innate courage buried within you.

INNER CRITIC *Maybe I'll think about doing this later.*

Procrastination is a lack of courage. You need courage;

> to take action
>
> to trust yourself
>
> to face difficulties
>
> to stay in the moment
>
> to grieve your losses
>
> to experience joy.
>
> to live a fulfilled life

INNER CRITIC *I think I'd prefer to stay in my comfort zone.*

It's up to you. It's your life. It actually takes courage to have an intention for your life. Sometimes it takes courage to remain engaged with life, even when it feels easier to withdraw into your comfort zone.

INNER CRITIC *Where does courage come from?*

It comes from the heart. It comes from taking action.

INNER CRITIC *Okay, so how do I get courage?*

You can experience courage by making a heart-felt intention for it to manifest in the days, months and years of your remaining life.

INNER CRITIC *That sounds daunting.*

To come through a challenge with courage is tremendously empowering. It gives you life-force and greater faith in yourself. A little courage can lead to more courage. With courage you can continue to explore new interests and foster a deeper connection with others.

In the late afternoon of life, it is especially beneficial to explore the quality of courage. It's an innate quality that you can choose to develop through intention. But courage on its own is not enough to ensure our well-being. To be courageous without wisdom can lead to disaster.

But before moving on, do you have time to take a few conscious breaths? It is possible to let go of the inner critic and find courage within the inhalation and the exhalation.

WISDOM

*The intention for my life is to be courageous and **(wise)**...*

Wisdom is the most positive quality generally associated with ageing, but just because you're old, it doesn't automatically follow that you will manifest wisdom.

Unlike knowledge, wisdom is not something that you can learn from others. It is more than common sense and good reasoning skills. It is not in some ancient scriptures or something a guru can give you. Wisdom comes from within and is based on a broad perspective on life with an innate understanding of the inter-connectedness of all things.

INNER CRITIC *I'm not wise.*

Which is why you need to make the intention to be wise.

INNER CRITIC *It sounds pretentious to call yourself wise. I'm not going to pretend.*

You are not pretending – it's just an intention to be wise. You may think of brilliant writers or academics as wise, but wisdom is not intelligence. You have an innate wisdom that is unique to you and your circumstances.

INNER CRITIC *I've made so many stupid mistakes in my life, I'm not suddenly going to become a wise person.*

No, you're not. However, if you plant in your mind a strong intention and nourish it, genuine wisdom will naturally emerge when you most need it.

INNER CRITIC *How will I know when I'm wise?*

Someone who labels themselves as wise, almost certainly isn't, but with all our imperfections and foibles, we can intend to be wise.

INNER CRITIC *So, what does wisdom look like?*

Wisdom can manifest in a thousand ways. In a single moment of time. In grief. In pain. In joy. In humour. In play. Wisdom may not be grand or conspicuous, but it can have long-term and profound effects on yourself and others.

Wisdom is a crucial element in navigating the challenges of ageing. Older people are often confronted with difficult decisions that have far-reaching consequences such as retirement planning, managing chronic illness, or making end-of-life choices. So much of modern life is about short-term thinking and instant gratification. There's an abundance of knowledge and information, but wisdom is in short supply.

Since ancient times, sages have believed wisdom and courage to be the two most essential qualities for well-being. They work together. Wisdom without courage is generally ineffective and courage without wisdom can lead to disaster.

So, what might it look like to have courage and wisdom in later life?

The invitation is to take a three conscious breaths. Enjoy the act of breathing. And three more deep breaths. Breath courage and wisdom into your life. Can you visualise yourself being wise and courageous as you grow older? Perhaps this is easy for you. Perhaps it is not possible at this stage, but keep going. Never give up! Keep breathing! Courage and wisdom are always there within you. Keep breathing and you will manifest them if that is your intention.

HEALING

*The intention for my life is to be courageous and wise in order to bring (**healing**)...*

With courage and wisdom all manner of things are possible. Might we want healing for ourselves and others?

INNER CRITIC *Why healing? We're not qualified. There are doctors and therapists for that.*

We expect doctors and therapists to cure symptoms but there's a dis-ease that is beyond the reach of medicine and therapy.

INNER CRITIC *What are you talking about?*

For many people, both young and old, there is an underlying sense of angst. Of not belonging. Of loss. Of unexpressed grief and disconnection to their true self..

INNER CRITIC *Everything is fine. I don't need healing.*

We are good at hiding our true feelings from others as well as ourselves. Today may be a good day. Tomorrow may be different. Later life can throw up all sorts of surprises. Both good and bad. Old age can be a reckoning where the causes of our past life become manifest effects.

Perhaps we don't know how to heal our wounds. but we can make the intention that our courage and wisdom will bring the healing that we need.

It is not just our own healing. In an inter-dependent world we are not separate from the suffering and inequality all around us. No matter how thick we build the walls of our castle, we are all inter-connected. 'As John Donne wrote;

No man is an island entire of itself; every man is a piece of the continent, a part of the main…

With famine, migration, war and environmental destruction in the news everyday, it may be tempting to pull up the drawbridge and just fend for yourself. But beware, such an attitude can easily lead to loneliness and isolation.

Of course, if you have a broken leg it is wise to see a professional but to believe that someone or something outside of ourselves can heal our deeper wounds is an illusion. Abdicating our responsibility just because we are no longer young, gives away our power.

JOY

*The intention for my life is to be courageous
and wise in order to bring healing and (**joy**)*

Courage, wisdom and healing are all very well, but we need more than worthy intentions. To live to an old age in piety is not enough. We need to experience the joy of being alive, otherwise what is the point of a long life?

INNER CRITIC *Joy? Do you mean happiness?*

No. Joy is an intense experience of positive emotion. Happiness is something else.

INNER CRITIC *So, I'd feel joy if I unexpectedly received a large sum of money.*

Not necessarily. You would probably feel rapture or happiness, but pure joy is not so connected to the material world.

INNER CRITIC *I'm not sure what you mean. How do I get joy?*

You can't plan to 'get' joy. It is not like a possession.

INNER CRITIC *Hmmm. I'm confused.*

Joy is mysterious and quixotic. It's spontaneous. It has an innocence to it.

INNER CRITIC *Now, I'm really confused..*

It's being fully alive in the present moment. It may be triggered by a piece of music, by a friend's arrival or even a passing cloud. Joy transcends the small self and reconnects the greater you to the inter-dependent universe.

INNER CRITIC *It doesn't sound like joy is going to be very useful in my life.*

Joy is the most precious of all treasures because moments of joy add up to more than the sum of their parts. So, as we grow older the moments of joy give a deep sense of appreciation for life and an inner peace.

Joy is the other side of the coin from grief. We cannot experience true joy if we supress our grief. As the revolutionary Buddhist monk, Nichiren Daishonin wrote over 800 years ago;

Suffer what there is to suffer, enjoy what there is to enjoy. Regard both suffering a joy as facts of life.

QUESTION 9

Take a few conscious breaths and clear your mind before answering the question below. See if you can bring to mind a moment of pure joy that you've experienced in your life. Try to find a spontaneous moment of joy that is not dependent on drugs, alcohol or material benefit. It may not be the most powerful experience, but whatever comes to mind right now.

Try to bring that moment to the front of your mind. What was it like? Can you begin to describe that specific moment?

What one moment of joy have you experienced in your life?

Do not be concerned if nothing comes to mind right now, but if something comes to mind later, write it down.

Some personal responses to QUESTION 9
"What one moment of joy have you experienced in your life?"

Standing on the top of a mountain in Wales in the early hours of a summer's morning with the sun coming up over the horizon.

Seeing the first seeds emerging from the soil

The first time I saw my partner's sleeping face

Joy often appears when I am cooking. The joy of the concoction. The smells. The tastes. It's divine chemistry!

I was standing under the pine trees looking up. Pigeons in the branches. Blue sky and fluffy clouds above. It was a moment. It was timeless. Eternal.

When I start a new painting and I have the empty canvass in front of me, I can feel both fear and joy. It's exhilarating.

Babies bring out joy. The innocence. I can't look at a baby without feeling joy.

MYSELF & OTHERS

*The intention for my life is to be courageous and wise in order to bring healing and joy to **(myself and others)***

A statement of intent will not be effective if it is not what you want for yourself. The intention must be something that you believe will be beneficial to you. However, as was mention earlier in the section about the Law of Attraction, an intention is more powerful if it includes the wellbeing of others.

INNER CRITIC *I want to see if this intention works for me first.*

From an inter-dependent perspective, you are not separate from others.

INNER CRITIC *Humans are essentially competitive and selfish creatures. I've been brought up to think about 'number one'.*

It's true that there is a highly competitive side to human nature, but empathy and cooperation are also a fundamental part of the human make-up.

Despite all the diets, skin creams, vitamins and exercise regimes, physical decline (entropy) is natural. This does not necessarily mean that our life needs to get smaller or close down before our final breath. We do not need to limit ourselves. Regardless of a lack of health or wealth, we can open up our hearts and minds to others in a way that was no possible when we were younger. By creating and committing to a clear intention for the wellbeing of ourselves and others, we will inevitably expand our lives. This is where the greatest joy will be found.

Planting the Seed of Intention

You may want to adopt the life-intention below word for word.

The intention for my life is to be wise and courageous in order to bring healing and joy to myself and others

Or you may wish to adapt it by changing some words

Or you may want to start from scratch and create a different life intention

It may be that you want to try out one or two different intentions. It is your choice. It's your life. If your intention is to be effective, you need to believe in it. Write the intention down. Play with the words. Try them out. It may take days or even weeks of trial and error but be persistent and keep going.

It is easy to put this process off and perhaps come back to it later in life. We know time flies so the sooner you plant the seed of intention in your life with commitment, the sooner the effects will emerge. Vagueness and procrastination will not bring results.

Memorise

Once you have decided on a form of words that works for you, it is important to memorise it. Check that you can bring the whole intention to mind at will. For some this may be easy to memorise their intention, although if this is a struggle for you, it is not a bad thing – working on it will help internalize it. Keep working on memorising your intention until it easily comes to mind. If you let the intention enter your heart, mind and soul, you will be surprised how the universe responds.

Question 10

You have prepared the ground. Now it is time to plant the seed in your life.

Take some deep breaths and clear your mind… Come into the present moment. Letting go of the busy-ness. Create space in the body and mind with each breath.

Watch your breath as you imagine that this present moment contains all your past moments … from the single cell zygote right up to this moment in time.

Keep watching your breath. Each breath is precious. The breath is sustaining you. All of the past is contained in each breath. You can't escape the past and there is no need to. Let go of any judgements. Right or wrong . Good or bad. Keep watching your breath.

Now take your mind to the final moment of your life. This is a moment that will inevitably come. You don't know when or how. That is not important right now. And take three deeper breaths. Relax your body. All is well. And breath normally.

Question 10 (cont)

Relax the jaw. Imagine a gentle smile on your lips. You are happy and at ease. Imagine that this moment right now contains your whole life. This moment contains the essence of who you are. From the single cell zygote right up to your final breath is contained in this precious moment.

This is a pivotal moment in your life. There is no hurry. You can relax. You can enjoy these breaths. You are content. When you are ready, bring your life-intention to mind. Remember each word as if it were a precious jewel. Carefully and deliberately write the answer to this question in your notebook.

What is the intention for your life?

Integrating Intention

Once you have committed your intention to memory, try saying it in your head in different situations and in different environments. Integrating your intention into your daily life might seem strange at first, but it will become second nature with practice. With a few conscious breaths, it is simple to bring the words of your intention to wherever you are. Silent connection with the words gives them power. It costs you nothing other than a few moments of time. All it requires is a little self-discipline. It relies on nothing outside of yourself. This is the practice of ageing consciously.

In the Morning and the Evening

Take 3 or more conscious breaths, then take a few moments to connect with the exact words that you have chosen for your life intention. It can become a habitual ritual like making a cup of tea after you wake up in the morning.

Plan to do this every day for the rest of your life no matter what the circumstances. There will be challenges and hard times but if you are consistent with this practice, it will transform the fear of ageing and death into meaningful connection and a powerful life force.

Tending the Shoots of Intention

Once you have established a consistent daily practice, there will be some key moments in your life when you can use the breathing and the life intention to bring transformation especially when you're;

- Not feeling confident eg when you're not sure that you have to courage to do something.

- Feeling anxious or fearful eg. In the doctor's waiting room

- Feeling lost, vulnerable, isolated or alone eg. 3am and unable to sleep

- Feeling impatient or waiting for something to happen eg waiting for a bus or a friend to arrive

At these times, take 3 or more conscious breaths, then take a few moments to connect with the exact words of your life intention.

Early days

Planting the seed of life intention is the opening up of a soulful connection to the universe, but it is a delicate process. Watch out for the judgmental part of you that demands perfection or the inner critic that says that whatever you do will not work out. Allow your intuitive self the freedom to work this process. There is an element of self-belief and faith in life that needs to happen.

Germination

If we have a sunflower seed, for example, but don't believe that a dried kernel weighing 0.05 grams can grow into a five foot radiant sunflower that contains over a thousand seeds, we probably wouldn't bother planting it. Sowing seeds requires a degree of trust in the power of nature. If we want the sunflower to grow into a healthy plant, then we should consider how best to plant it. The soil, wind and the amount of sunlight are important factors. And once planted, it needs watering and a little care before the benefit of planting the seed is realised Most seeds germinate in darkness and they take time. In a world where we can access information and buy things we want in seconds, beware of impatience. You may expect to see some results from your intention within days. It might seem as though nothing is happening, but the gestation period for the intention is crucial. It needs to bed into your mind and soul. It has to take root. Again, this takes some awareness and trust. The more you commit to your intention, the more precious it becomes. The words you have chosen are yours. Own them. You might want to keep them to yourself, or you might choose to tell others. Think carefully before sharing your intention. It is wise not to be flippant but to guard your life intention with care, and if you do share it with another, make sure that they are able to respect your commitment. Your life intention is not up for debate or superficial chat.

Doubts

Of course, there will be days when you do not live up to the intention. Fear may lead to self- doubt and down the rabbit hole of denial, distractions or dysfunctional behaviour. There will be times when your intended qualities and values do not emerge in your life. You will probably have doubts about the efficacious merits of your intention. Perhaps you have the wrong intention? Perhaps you are just not good enough or you have set the bar too high?

When you feel doubt, weak or foolish, keep breathing consciously and re-determine to connect your intention. This is what gives you power. As Mahatma Gandhi said;

Your struggles develop your strengths. When you go through hardships and decide not to surrender, that is strength.

Commitment to a life intention creates on-going transformation. It does not bring perfection. You can't be your best self all of the time. Sometimes your negative or shadow side will win through. Instead of feeling courageous, you may feel weak and start to doubt yourself. Sometimes unresolved issues from the past can emerge and throw us off course, as in the case of Justin;

JUSTIN'S EXPERIENCE

Justin had some turbulent times as a young adult, but was fortunate enough to get some support and guidance in his thirties. It enabled Justin to stabilised his life, start a family and built up a successful design business.

When Justin was 53, his father died, and he was surprised by how affected he was by the death. There had been plenty of animosity between the two of them, but after the funeral, Justin started drinking like he used to thirty years ago. He was shocked at the pain he felt, and in the mornings after, he was appalled by his own lack of self-control. When he let down one of his long standing clients with some crucial launch designs, the shame was crippling and it seemed there was no way out of the downward spiral.

Fortunately, Helen ,the client that he had let down, saw beyond her own disappointment and felt concern for her designer who was normally so reliable. Helen ended up supporting Justin in finding a healthy way to accept his loss. It took a while but Justin came to realise that his grief was not just for the loss of his father. The grief was for the lack of love he received as a child.

After some reflection, Justin felt able to accept the pain rather than push it away. The grief was still there but there was also a new sense of freedom. He reconnected with the intentions he had made in his thirties and let go of some of the heavy baggage he had been carrying since he was a child.

Justin was fortunate to have a wise and compassionate client who was not just concerned with her own immediate needs, but was able to see a bigger picture in a time of crisis. Without commitment and intention in later life it is easy to stagnate and slowly drift into a place of hellish isolation which is what happened to Charlotte's sister.

CHARLOTTE & ANN'S EXPERIENCE (Continued)

Charlotte went round to visit her sister, Ann, on her seventy-fifth birthday and was shocked by the deterioration in her sister's health and spirits. Ann's home was as unkempt as its owner. Charlotte started on the backlog of dirty dishes in the sink before Ann started shouting at her sister to get out of her house. Charlotte couldn't understand why Ann was so angry and resentful about growing old. It was deeply upsetting for Charlotte who used to share so much with her sister.

Tending the Fruit of Intention

Over the months, years and possibly decades, working with a strong life intention will become an integral part of who you are. Despite set-backs, you will naturally be able to transform your worries and doubts about the future into a deepening sense of self and inner freedom. Your innate wisdom will enable you to discern what serves you and what does not. There will still be difficulties but you will be better equipped to turn challenges into benefits. You will stop carrying the rucksack of doubt and regret, so that you can enter later life with a profound sense of fulfilment.

No matter how difficult (or easy) your circumstances may be, a commitment to breath and intention will integrate your past and your future with the present moment.

In Ralph's case, it was in the worst of times that he found the seed of an inner peace.

RALPH'S EXPERIENCE (Continued)

After being made redundant from the Sixth Form College, Ralph fell to pieces. He had terrible rows with his sister who told him some uncomfortable home truths. His mother was slowly dying in a care home and then his wife left him for a younger man. It was the perfect storm for Ralph, and it forced him to review his life and come to term with his mortality.

Ralph who had had two short stories published in his 20s, realized that in nearly thirty years of teaching literature at the college, he had written nothing but reports. While he was documenting his personal transformation in a journal, Ralph started to explore his writing further, and discovered a sense of joy and freedom that had been missing all these years. He enjoyed writing and no longer felt that he had to prove himself.

Today, many things have changed in Ralph's life. He has slowed down. Every day he breathes with intention. He lives on a tight budget, so the car, the overseas holidays, the frequent meals out have all gone. All the things that he thought were crucial for his happiness are no longer available to him but, surprisingly, Ralph feels that he has finally come fully into his own.

Every week he spends time with his mother. Despite her worsening condition, Ralph finds a deep gratitude to the woman who gave him life.

The transformation that Ralph experienced is not uncommon around retirement. It is a difficult transition from one life stage to another – as precarious as the passage from adolescence to adulthood.

What's Our Legacy?

In indigenous societies there is a distinction made between an "elder" and an "older" person. Elders are respected for their wisdom and courage. They're initiated into a sacred role of protecting the values and stories of their tribe. They hold the long view for the tribes well-being. Today most of us in the West have no tribe. We get a bus pass and a pension and there is no initiation. We have many 'olders' who wonder what is going on and we have few empowered elders.

It is a time honoured tradition that older people moan about the state of the world to anyone who will listen. We can conform to this stereotype by expressing our righteous indignation, but our opinions will change nothing. We can tell people about *how it was in our day* and can sink into nostalgia about the good times when we were young, but generally it leads us into a sad, lonely shell.

So, how can we take the long view? The development of technology and Artificial Intelligence is so rapid, few people have any idea of what our society will look like by the end of the decade. How can we support and foster future generations who face an uncertain future with the growing threat of environmental destruction, mass migration and nuclear war. As inter-dependent adults we are connected to the greed, anger and stupidity of the political elite. We are not separate from the suffering.

After mid-life, there may be a temptation to say; *I have done my bit. I deserve to put my feet up and enjoy the rest of my life.* You may think that most of humanity is doomed. Your inner critic may think it ridiculous that we have the power to change anything in later life. You may be believe that it is best to go quietly into your twilight years. Perhaps you think that the best we can hope for is minimal pain and a little solace as we part this burning planet.

However, there are many examples of a fundamental social change stemming for a few 'powerless' pioneers. If you had asked a hundred years ago, if women could have equal rights as men, most would have been unable to even imagine such a thing. A similar change in consciousness happened with gay rights. In our lifetime, homosexuality was seen as a disease for which you could be imprisoned. It took a few courageous pioneers to believe that change was possible.

In our lifetime, the prevailing ethic within the medical profession was that patients should be cured and if that wasn't possible then it was regarded as failure. It was acceptable to lie to patients about their prognosis until one nurse by the name of Cecily Saunders thought people at the end of their lives should be given effective pain management. She insisted that dying people needed dignity, compassion, and respect. In 1967 she founded first hospice that started a movement that has spread all over the world. She and a few other pioneers such as Elizabeth Kubler-Ross have had a huge impact on how we think about death and dying. It is a change in consciousness that few could have predicted.

A fundamental shift in consciousness around ageing is possible and is absolutely necessary for the foundation of a healthy and peaceful society. If older people can transform the fear of ageing into meaningful connection and purpose, then there would be less terror in the world and a greater appreciation for all stages of life as well as for nature itself.

By ageing without fear we can naturally give courage to others. As elders-in-training we do not need to fix, rescue or advise. By being in the present moment and breathing with clear and strong intention, we can model the power in ageing. We can inspire each other as well as give hope to younger generations.

PART 3

NOTES

147 The Life-Stage Community

151 Being with Age

159 Practical Planning for End of Life

165 Thanks

157 Acknowledgements

167 Further reading

THE LIFE-STAGE COMMUNITY

Life-Stage facilitates regular talks and free on-line discussions as well as workshops and courses on *The Power in Ageing*. It also enables staff and residents in retirement organisations to facilitate courses.

If you would like to find out more about some of the topics discussed in this book you can become a member of the growing Life-Stage community for free at www.life-stage.org

You will receive a regular newsletter with information about Life-Stage talks, events, on-line courses, workshops and one-to-one sessions.

Since November 2021, Life-Stage's facilitators have held open discussion on some of the important topics around later life. Participants listen and share without trying to fix, rescue or advise others. The 90 minute sessions are free.

If you have any feedback or questions about the book, please email info@life-stage.org

LIFE-STAGE MONTHLY FORUMS

Below are some of the topics the Life-Stage community have discussed over the past two years;

- What does resilience mean to you?
- How can we live in healthy community in later life?
- How have you processed loss?
- Have you internalise ageist beliefs?
- Who or what inspires you in later life?
- How can we remain curious and creative in later life?
- Asking for help – what's your experience?
- What attachments might it be useful to let go of?
- Is a sense of purpose essential in later life?
- How do you develop friendships in later life?

Experienced facilitators encourage participants to talk about their own thoughts and feelings while not judging those expressed by others in the group.

Email info@life-stage.org for free link to monthly online forum

BEING WITH AGE

Even with limited resources and mobility, there are certain activities that can strongly support inter-dependence and resilience in later life. There are a few suggestions here, many of which you may already participate in.

Regular Practice

This is about creating time and space for yourself without external interruption. It may be meditation, prayer, chanting, breathing or mindfulness. It may involve some physicality such as yoga or chi gung. It is a time for you to step away from the demands of modern life and to connect with your true nature. To do this on a daily basis and combine it with a deep awareness of your life-intention is empowering.

Nature

Being connected to the natural world is a reminder of our inter-dependence. Whether it is walking in the woods, gardening, swimming in the sea or simply being in the park, it has great benefit and is important for our mental health. To be conscious of the life of birds, insects, trees and plants can bring wonder and to gratitude. Nature and the seasons remind us of transience, ageing, death and renewal. Regular connect with nature reminds us that at our core we are not separate entities.

Creativity

This may be singing, playing, writing, dancing, cooking or painting. Talking and dialogue can be creative or it can be functional and formulaic. Spontaneous expression without the fear of being judged by yourself or others can be challenging. It maybe that we have to confront the fear of the unknown - the blank page or canvas for example. To be creative in whatever way takes a kind of courage. To do it without the need for recognition can bring moments of great connection and joy.

Open Communication

For some of us, the second half of life is an opportunity to be true to ourselves in a way that maybe wasn't possible when we were younger. Hopefully we have more freedom to communicate what we really feel. The language of independence and separation is often perfunctory. A friend asks if you're okay and it's easier and socially more acceptable to say *I'm fine, thanks* than to express a feeling. It can be seen as anti-social or even rude to answer honestly. It's what we have always done - taken the easiest or most efficient route. It's understandable when you're struggling for survival in the busy world, but as we increasingly realise our time on this planet is finite, so we can be clearer about our true feelings. It can be surprising, uncomfortable or even shocking for those around you who are still expecting the social niceties. Expressing our true feelings makes us vulnerable to the judgments and criticism of others. It takes practice but it is empowering.

Dyads

Perhaps we don't know what we're feeling or how to express our feelings. Dyads are a wonderful process that cost nothing and need only takes around 20 minutes. It can be done face-to-face or on-line with a friend, a relative or with anyone you feel safe to confide in.

Both parties start by agreeing that nothing that said is to be repeated outside of the session. Confidentiality is important as there needs to be a strong degree of trust. One of you ask the first question of the other, 'How are you feeling physically?' This is your chance to answer spontaneously by checking in with yourself in that moment. The more open and vulnerable you are with your reply the better. If you stumble or are lost for words, it doesn't matter. When you have explored your physical well-being or lack of it, you conclude by saying, "That's how I'm feeling physically'. This might take two or three minutes. Your dyad partner listens <u>without judgement and makes no comments</u>, and then asks the next question (see below). Once you have answered the four questions below, you may thank your friend and then reverse roles and it's your turn to ask the questions. This format allows the speaker to explore how they are in the moment without analysis and it allows the listener to connect empathically.

Dyad Questions

1. How are you feeling physically?

Eg. Health. Energy levels. Sense of the physicality. Active. Tired.

2. How are you feeling mentally?

Eg. Interests. Intellectual engagement. Involvement with ideas. Learning. Reading.

3. How are you feeling emotionally?

Eg. Angry. Sad. Connected. Loving. Lonely. Anxious.

4. How are you feeling about spiritually?

Eg. A chance to honestly explore the deeper aspect of your life.

Death Awareness

Throughout history, cultures have known how potent an awareness of death can be. Socrates encouraged his students to practice the art of dying. In ancient Japan there was a code of ethics for the fierce Samurai warriors[1] that read;

"...morning after morning, the practice of death, considering whether it will be here or be there, imagining the most sightly way of dying, and putting one's mind firmly in death. Although this may be a most difficult thing, if one will do it, it can be done. There is nothing that one should suppose cannot be done"

In earlier days Christians would remind themselves of their mortality with *memento mori*[2] - literally, reminders of death. Artists would be paid by their wealthy patrons to heighten their awareness of the transience of life with skulls and images of decay in their paintings. Today, for many people life is so busy that they get little time to consider their mortality. The consumer society has the power to distract us from such vital issues as ageing and death. There are endless virtual entertainments that might prevent us from looking at the reality of our existence. But as we get older the health of relatives and friends starts to deteriorate and it becomes harder to ignore the fact that we have limited time on this earth.

Considering our own death with a resolute mind is crucial if we are to transform the fear into meaningful connection and purpose. Some say it doesn't matter how you die. It's the end of the story and that is that, but as Atul Gawande[14] wrote, *'We all want to be the authors of our own stories, and in stories endings matter'*.

Death Cafe

At a Death Café people gather to eat cake, drink tea and talk about death. The objective is to increase

---

14 *Being Mortal: Illness, Medicine and What Matters in the End* Profile Books 2015

awareness of death with a view to helping people make the most of their finite lives. A death cafe is a group directed discussion of death with no agenda, objectives or themes. It is a discussion group rather than a grief support or counselling session. Death cafes have spread quickly across Europe North America and Australasia. There have been over 18,000 death cafes in 85 countries since 2011. Although people may be strangers and from very different walks of life there is no shortage of things to talk about. Far from being a depressing experience, a Death Café generally leaves people feeling invigorated. There is humour, vulnerability and honest connection.

You can find out where the next death cafe is in a location close to you by going to www.deathcafe.com. If there is not one in your area, it is easy to start your own.

Acknowledging Grief

Since Elizabeth Kubler-Ross [3] wrote her book 'The Five Stages of Grief' in 1969, many books have been written and much academic research undertaken into the subject. It's a complicated picture with many theories and no quick fix solutions. Of course, grief in some cases can lead to chronic dysfunction and may require specialist counselling. But, finding a healthy way to acknowledge our loss and the grief can be healing in the present and can enable us the celebrate the joy of living more fully.

The well-known psychotherapist, Frances Weller, suggests that there are 'five gates of grief'.

1 All that we love we will lose

2 The places in us that did not receive love

3 The sorrows of the world

4 What we expected but did not receive

5 Ancestral grief

Frances Weller's book, *The Wild Edge of Sorrow*, "offers precious guidance into acknowledging grief

PLANNING FOR END OF LIFE

There are some practical actions that we would be wise to consider as we grow older. Not only will this be supportive to you later on but may also be helpful for those that care for you. The following notes are based on material kindly provided by Sarah Goodman, an End of Life Doula.

Advance Statement

An Advance Statement allows you to make general statements, describing your wishes and preferences about future care should you be unable to make or communicate a decision or express your preferences at the time. You may want it to reflect religious or other beliefs and important aspects of your life. You can include things such as food and drink preferences; type of clothes you like to wear; music, TV or DVD preferences, or whether you like a bath or a shower etc. You can say who you would like to visit you or be consulted about your care.

It is not legally binding but should be taken into account when those who are taking care of you are considering your best interests. There are no formal guidelines for making an Advance Statement but it's a good idea to write your name, date of birth and address on the document and to also sign and date it. Including your personal information and signature helps to confirm that it's your wishes that are written down.

You can also use it to specify any people you'd like to be consulted – Proxy Spokes Person/People – when decisions are being made on your behalf. However, doing this doesn't mean that a healthcare professional has to follow what that person says. The only way to give another person the legal power to make health or care decisions on your behalf is by making a Lasting Power of Attorney

Advance Decision to Refuse Treatment

An advance decision to refuse treatment also known as an advance decision, an ADRT, or a living will is a decision you can make now to refuse a specific type of treatment at some time in the future should you lose mental capacity e.g. severe dementia, a stroke etc. Examples of treatments which can be refused include, but are not limited to Cardiopulmonary Resuscitation, Mechanical or Artificial Ventilation, Artificial Nutrition and Hydration and Antibiotics. It is legally binding and to be valid must be made when the person has mental capacity and be signed, dated and witnessed. It must include the words I maintain this refusal even if my life is at risk or shortened as a result.

Do Not Attempt Cardiopulmonary Resuscitation (DNACPR)

A Do Not Attempt Cardio Pulmonary Resuscitation form is a document issued and signed by a doctor, which tells your medical team not to attempt cardiopulmonary resuscitation (CPR). It's not a legally binding document. Instead, it helps you to communicate to the healthcare professionals involved in your care that CPR shouldn't be attempted. If you decide to have one, it's a good idea to also to make this a refusal in your advance decision. This will mean that your wishes are more likely to be followed if you lack capacity to make decisions.

Treatment Escalation Plan (TEP)

TEPs are in operation in some NHS Trusts. It includes both treatments you may and may not want. A TEP form is a way of your doctor recording your individual treatment plan, focusing on which treatments she/he believes may or may not be most helpful for you. A variety of treatments can be considered, such as antibiotics, artificial feeding or ventilation of your lungs. It is not legally binding. It is important that you ensure that your Doctor has consulted with you regarding the completion of the form so that you understand it and it reflects what you want.

Lasting Power of Attorney (LPA)

A Lasting Power of Attorney (LPA) allows you to give someone you trust the legal power to make decisions on your behalf in case you later become unable to make decisions for yourself. The person who makes the LPA is known as the 'donor' and the person given the power to make decisions is known as the 'attorney'.

There are two different types of LPA: 1. An LPA for Property and Financial Affairs covers decisions about money and property. 2. An LPA for Health and Welfare covers decisions about health and personal welfare. You can choose to have just an Advance Decision to Refuse Treatment, just an LPA for Health & Welfare, or both. An LPA for Health & Welfare is broader in remit than an Advance Decision (it can include care arrangements, dietary preferences, etc). It can cover the same ground insofar as it addresses your refusals of treatment. If you choose to have both an Advance Decisions and an LPA for Health & Welfare it is important to ensure that they work together and that one does not invalidate the other.

LPAs can be undertaken by a Solicitor or can be done by you on-line at the Gov UK website https://www.gov.uk/power-of-attorney/overview.

Proxy Spokes Person/People

For when decisions are being made on your behalf should you lack capacity. These would be a person/people with whom you have communicated your wishes choices and preferences. However, doing this doesn't mean that a healthcare professional has to follow what that person says. The only way to give another person the legal power to make health or care decisions on your behalf is by making a Lasting Power of Attorney.

Funerals

There is useful information on all the options and choices available at:
https://www.goodfuneralguide.co.uk/

Wills

There is no requirement for a will to be drawn up or witnessed by a solicitor so an individual can make a will themselves. It is certainly advisable though to use a solicitor to make sure it will have the effect you want.

Digital Legacy

This is the consideration of what you want to happen with your all your accounts, blogs, social networking identities and digital files that will be left online when you die.

Organ and Tissue Donation

https://www.organdonation.nhs.uk/
Whole Body Donation
https://www.hta.gov.uk/donating-your-body

Notes based on material kindly provided by Sarah Goodman, an End of Life Doula.

THANKS

This book would not have been possible without the on-going encouragement and support from Simon Chinnery. His faith and guidance has kept the Life-Stage project alive. I have gratitude to Eleni Xenophontos and to Jamie Martin for editorial advice and corrections. I also thank Nicola Glinwood, Cathy Warren, Ben Cole, Spencer Thomas, and Felice Rhiannon from the Life-Stage Core Group for their on-going engagement.

I'm grateful to Michael Roberts who helped set up the first on-line course in Earlsdon Retirement Village as well as to Jenny Kirton and Joanna Frances who ran Life-Stage courses for other residents in their community.

Thanks to Roger Ross who helped out at difficult time. Tim Rabjohns for media support and guidance, and to Nigel Ribeiro for tech. support. Several people gave useful feedback on an early draft including Claudius Hillman, Brian Donovan, and Gail Davidson.

Finally, thanks to Sally Garrett who gave me the space and understanding to complete the book.

FURTHER READING

Applewhite, Ashton. *This Chair Rocks: A Manifesto Against Ageism* Celadon Books, 2020

Becker, Ernest. *The Denial of Death*. New York: Free Press 1973

Hillman, James. *The Soul's Code* Random House 1996

Hollis, James. *The Middle Passage: From Misery to Meaning in Mid Life*. Toronto: Inner City Books, 1993

Ikeda, Daisaku; Saito, Katsuji; Endo, Takanori; Suda, Haruo *The Wisdom of the Lotus Sutra. Vol. 1*. World Tribune Press 2000

James, John. W; Friedman, Russell. *The Grief Recovery Handbook*. William Morrow Paperbacks 2017

Jenkinson, Stephen. *Die Wise: A Manifesto for Sanity and Soul*. North Atlantic Books, 2015

Kübler-Ross, Elisabeth. *On Death and Dying*. Scribner, 2014

Levine, Stephen. *Healing into Life and Death*. Anchor, 1989

Macy, Joanna; Brown, Molly Young. *Coming Back to Life*. New Society Publishers, 2014

Mannix, Dr. Kathryn. *With the End in Mind*. William Collins 2019

Moody, Harry R.; Carroll, David. *The Five Stages of the Soul*. Anchor, 1998

Pevny, Ron. *Conscious Living Conscious Aging*. Atria Books, 2014

Plotkin, Bill. *Nature and the Human Soul*. New World Library., 2008

Ram Dass, Ram; Bush, Miraba. *Walking Each Other Home: Conversations on Loving and Dying*. Sounds True, 2018

Rhiannon, Felice. *Ageing with Awareness* www.elder-spirit.co.uk, 2023

Schachter-Sahlomi, Zalman; Miller Ronald S. *From Ageing to Sageing: A Revolutionary Approach to Growing Older*. Grand Central Publishing, 2014

Weller, Frances *The Wild Edge of Sorrow* North Atlantic Books 2015

Printed in Great Britain
by Amazon